5 50

D0915734

LENA HORNE

LENA HORNE

James Haskins

Coward-McCann, Inc.
New York

Designed by Cecily Dunham
Second printing
Printed in the United States of America

Library of Congress Cataloging in Publication Data
Haskins, James,
  Lena Horne.
  Includes index.
  1. Horne, Lena. 2. Singers—United States—
Biography. 1. Title.
ML420.H65H4   1983   784.5'0092'4 [B]   83-15411
ISBN 0-698-20586-3

Contents

1   *Well-born in Brooklyn*   11

2   *Life on the Road*   18

3   *Lena Goes to Work*   27

4   *Teenage Bride*   41

5   *Back in Show Business*   51

6   *On Her Own*   59

7   *Lena Moves to Hollywood*   70

8   *Battling Hollywood Prejudice*   84

9   *Lena and Lennie Marry*   98

10   *Lena on Broadway*   111

11   *Civil Rights Activist*   125

12   *Tragedy and Renewal*   136

13   *Lena Horne: Legend*   147

    Index   155

Acknowledgments

I am grateful to Elza Dinwiddie, Joan "Halimah" Brooks, and Kathy Benson for their help.

LENA HORNE

1
Well-born in Brooklyn

*L*ena Calhoun Horne was born on June 30, 1917, in Brooklyn, New York. Her mother, Edna Scottron Horne, went to a small Jewish hospital to give birth to her first, and only, child. *Her* mother-in-law, Cora Calhoun Horne, went with her. Both women were so light-complected that the hospital staff assumed they were white. When the copper-colored Lena arrived, the surprised nurses took the infant all over the hospital, showing her off.

Although the infant Lena was much too young to understand what all the fuss was about, from the time she was old enough to understand color differences she would be aware of the importance of skin color in the world. It was especially important in the community into which Lena was born. The Horne family was prominent in Brooklyn's black middle class. Like their white counterparts, this small, intensely proud group of black doctors, lawyers, schoolteachers, funeral directors, government and social workers shared a desire for material comforts and sought nice homes and clothes. They held a respect for social convention, and an esteem for personal ambition. They also prized Caucasianlike physical characteristics such as fair skin and straight hair.

Back in 1917, when Lena was born, prejudice and racial segregation were so strong and tradition-bound that even black people themselves had a color consciousness. Like their white fellow Americans, many black people gave preferential treatment to the lighter-skinned members of their own race. They scorned the term *black* and preferred the words *Negro* or *colored*. They had found that lighter-skinned Negroes had an easier time of it in a predominantly white society, and somehow that fact had been translated into the idea that lighter-skinned Negroes were somehow better than their darker-complected fellows.

This color consciousness was partly a holdover from slavery, when the slaves who were given the easier jobs in the "big house" often had lighter complexions than those who had to do hard labor in the fields. White slave masters fathered children by female slaves, producing a lighter-skinned, usually favored, caste of slaves. This deeply rooted color favoritism continued among both blacks and whites after slavery was abolished. Lighter-skinned Negroes also had an easier time as freemen, enjoying greater acceptance from whites and thus greater opportunities for education and entry into various professions. The Negro community, like any other community, held its professionals in high esteem. Remnants of this color consciousness exist today in the minds of both blacks and whites.

Lena Horne inherited her copper-colored complexion from her father, Teddy Horne, who was among the darker-skinned members of the Horne family. Like most families that made up the Brooklyn black middle class, the Hornes had a range of skin colors, and color was not the only reason for their prominence in the community. Most of them were good-looking, well-educated, refined people who were active in local affairs and who claimed their middle-classdom with ease. Teddy Horne's father, Edwin, Lena's paternal grandfather, was an intellectual. Teddy's mother, Cora, Lena's paternal grandmother, was active in the Ethical Culture movement, whose belief was that "the supreme aim of human life is working to create a more humane society." She was also a fervent fighter for the civil and human rights that in those days were called "Negro causes."

Besides being darker skinned than his parents or his three brothers, Teddy Horne did not share his parents' interests (and perhaps there was a connection between the two). He didn't like school and at age eight took it upon himself to get a job across the river in Manhattan, as a hotel page boy. Naturally, his parents put a stop to that when they found out. But Teddy Horne had already demonstrated an independence that was not common in the Brooklyn middle class. As he grew older, he showed a liking for gambling and socializing that was not approved of in that small, proud community.

He did at least marry a young woman from the community. Edna Scottron's mother had attended the only Negro teacher-training school in Brooklyn, and Edna was pampered by both her mother and grandmother. She dreamed of a career as an actress, which also wasn't approved of in the community, and she was probably attracted to Teddy Horne because of his independence. But when they were married she really was not ready for the responsibility of being a wife. For that matter, Teddy Horne was equally ill-prepared for his responsibilities as a husband.

When Teddy and Edna got married, they did not have enough money to start a household of their own, so they moved in with Teddy's parents. Lena was born, and the young family continued to stay on in the Horne house. It was difficult for Lena's parents to establish a life of their own when they were living in the house of others, especially a household dominated by the stern Cora

Calhoun Horne. And that was just one of the problems. Lena's father remained as independent as ever. Lena's mother wanted to be pampered as much as ever. Lena was about three years old when her parents' marriage broke up. She does not remember exactly when or why her father left, but suddenly he was not there anymore. Following his dream of independence, Teddy Horne went West, gambling and working his way, and periodically sending back money for his family.

For a while after her husband left, Edna Scottron Horne remained in her in-laws' home. After a time, Edna decided she could no longer live with her domineering mother-in-law. She had dreams to follow, too, just as her husband did. Her dream was to be an actress. She believed acting was in her blood because there had been two people in her grandfather's family who had passed for white and gone into show business. Promising that she would come back to get Lena when she was able to do so, she, too, left her small daughter.

Lena stayed on in the Horne house on Chauncey Street, with her grandfather, Edwin, her grandmother, Cora, and her uncle, Burke, her father's youngest brother, who was still in school. Although some of the tension in the household had lifted when first Teddy and then Edna had gone, there was still plenty of it left over. Lena now became more aware of the strain in her grandparents' marriage. They slept in separate bedrooms and rarely spoke to one another except to say "good morning" and "good evening." When they had something more to say, they wrote notes, which their son Burke carried back and forth between them.

Occupied with her work and civic activities, Cora Calhoun Horne had little interest in cooking or cleaning. Edwin Horne made his own breakfast. Young Uncle Burke cooked oatmeal for Lena in the morning before they left for school. Since it was her grandfather's habit to start a fire in the furnace early on a cold winter morning, by the time Lena joined her uncle in the kitchen it would be warm and cozy.

As a young girl, Lena thought that her grandfather was a very beautiful man. She liked his gray mustache, gray hair, sparkling blue eyes. She also sensed that he was very lonely, and she was drawn to him. Both of them needed a friend. Her grandfather responded to her caring, and the two of them became constant companions. They went to museums, the zoo, the aquarium, movie matinees. They often lunched at the Automat when they went out. Back home, Edwin Horne played records for Lena, introducing her to black Shakespearean actors and to the great black singers of the time, like Florence Mills.

On Sundays, Lena and her grandfather often spent the entire day together. Her grandmother was in the habit of spending the day in bed resting after a long week that included her full-time job as a social worker with delinquent boys in Harlem and her evening activities with the National Association for the Advancement of Colored People, the Ethical Culture Society, and the movement for women's voting rights. Downstairs in the front room, Edwin Horne sat in his favorite chair smoking aromatic Havana cigars and reading the *New York Times*. He usually had the music of Giuseppi Verdi on the record player. Lena sprawled on the floor in front of the bookcase, leafing through books. In the early afternoon, the two walked hand in hand to a nearby delicatessen to get Sunday dinner. They often got two or three other meals during the week from the delicatessen as well, since no one in the Horne family liked to cook. After collecting an assortment of potato salad, baked beans, cold cuts, kosher dill pickles, and other delicatessen offerings, Lena and her grandfather would spread their Sunday feast out on the kitchen table and have fun sampling a bit of everything.

Lena heard little from her parents during this period of her life and saw even less of them. Her father kept in touch more regularly than her mother did. He sent her a fur coat, toys, clothes, letters, and pretty picture postcards from the places where he traveled. Lena's grandmother would take the time to talk with Lena about the things her father sent her and about his journeys. Lena's mother, utterly intimidated by her mother-in-law, wrote Lena less often. She probably suspected that each letter that arrived from her was an occasion for Cora Calhoun Horne to scorn her daughter-in-law for pursuing an empty dream at the expense of the little girl she had left behind. And if Edna Horne was hesitant even to write letters, she was even more lacking in the will to brave her mother-in-law and visit Lena. Lena remembers seeing her mother only occasionally during those years. Edna Horne was working as an actress with the Lafayette Players, a black stock company connected with the Lafayette Theatre in Harlem that toured the East Coast. She was often out of town and unable to visit her daughter. When she was in town, she sometimes could not summon the courage. One furtive visit stands out in Lena's mind. She was playing in the yard when a neighbor called her over to the gate that separated the two properties. There on the other side of the gate stood her mother, who hugged and kissed her, promised that they would be together soon, and then left.

When Lena reached school age, she enrolled in the Brooklyn Ethical Culture School, sponsored by the Cora Calhoun Horne Scholarship. She also participated in other activities of her grandmother's, for Cora Calhoun Horne was determined to raise her granddaughter in the manner she considered proper—as an aware, articulate, educated young lady. Lena attended meetings of the NAACP and other organizations to which her grandmother belonged. Always, she was the only child there. She had to listen attentively so that after the meetings she could answer her grandmother's questions about what she had heard. Her grandmother chose the friends she could play with, too. The Chauncey

Street neighborhood was a racially mixed one, and Lena was not allowed to play with any white children. Potential black friends were judged according to Cora Calhoun Horne's strict standards of behavior and deportment, and so some of these children were off-limits to Lena as well, since they did not measure up to her grandmother's expectations.

After a day at the Ethical Culture School, Lena had to go straight home; she could not stop to play with her classmates. She would arrive home to find herself alone, most of the time, everyone else being out, but she could not go over to a neighbor's to play. She had to stay in her own yard. Often, she would entertain herself by dressing up in her grandmother's elegant clothes and play-acting, her favorite game. This usually kept her entertained and occupied until the rest of the family came home for dinner and the evening's activities.

One day Lena was all dressed up in some of her grandmother's fine clothes and playing in the family's front yard. Suddenly, a head appeared above the shiny black iron fence that shielded the yard from the street and from the neighbors. It was her mother's cousin, Augusta, who told Lena that she had come to take her to Manhattan to visit her mother. Lena ran into the house to change her clothes, then rushed back outside to join Cousin Augusta for the trip to Manhattan.

Much of Lena's excitement evaporated when she found her mother sick in bed. In a weak voice, her mother told her that she had to take her away from her grandparents' house because her father planned to go back there and kidnap her. From then on, she and her mother would be together. She would not be going back to the house on Chauncey Street.

2

Life on the Road

In Brooklyn, despite the strains in the Horne household and the loneliness of not having either a mother or a father at home, Lena had at least been part of a family and a member of a community. She had a home, a place to return to every day. She had a name that meant something in the Brooklyn community. She knew who she was, where she had come from, and, to some extent, where she was headed. When she was seven, her mother took her away from all that.

The life Lena's mother led was not at all stable. In those days, very few entertainers enjoyed settled lives. Even the talented ones spent a great deal of time on the road, traveling to where the work was. This was especially true for black entertainers, whose jobs were few and far between. Edna Horne had not had any formal training in acting, and apparently she did not have much talent. Her good looks kept her in show business for as long as she managed to remain in the field. Her dreams of becoming a star were dreams only; she would remain an obscure traveling actress, moving from place to place, staying in rooming houses, eating when there was enough money for food. At first, Lena was so happy to be with her mother again that she did not care about such things, but as they began to travel she found that she missed the stability of life in Brooklyn.

Not long after Cousin Augusta took her from her grandparents' house, Lena and her mother left New York for Philadelphia, where Edna thought there was work. They stayed in Philadelphia only briefly, then left for Miami, Florida, where Edna had been promised a job. Edna packed all their belongings and bundled her young daughter up and together they boarded a Florida-bound train. Apparently suffering from rheumatism, Edna was in a great deal of misery during the trip; every lurch of the train intensified her pain.

Lena recalls being fed and cuddled to sleep by two or three heavyset, dark-skinned black women who realized that her mother was not in any shape to take care of her. Lena had encountered quite a few strangers in the brief time she had been with her mother, but this was the first time she had ever experienced such kindness from people she did not know. Since she was frightened and lonely, she was especially grateful for their caring, and she would remember that train trip with a mixture of emotions.

It was also on that train trip that she encountered segregation for the first time. Once the train reached the South, all the Negro people had to move to "Jim Crow" cars. Once they reached Miami, there was more segregation to deal with. The main thing Lena remembers is that her shoes always hurt. In Miami in the 1920s black people were not allowed to try on shoes in shoe stores; they had to buy them and hope they would fit.

In Miami, Lena's mother's rheumatism continued to pain her so much that she had to hire a woman to take care of her and her daughter. This woman gave Lena her first beatings. She would hit Lena over the most trivial thing, warning her not to do anything that would disturb or upset her "poor sick mother." She demanded that Lena be on her very best behavior all the time and admonished her that she must always be "good" for her mother.

Since Lena had been reared by her grandmother to be an extremely well-behaved child, she could not understand the vicious physical abuse from this woman. But she was afraid to upset her mother by telling her about the beatings. She tried doubly hard to be good, hoping that she could avoid the beatings that way, but she never seemed to be able to be good enough.

Despite her rheumatism, Edna Horne did have guaranteed work in Miami, and she and Lena spent several months there. Lena enrolled in a local elementary school, and it was a far cry from the Ethical Culture School back in Brooklyn. It was an all-black school, because schools were segregated in Miami. It consisted of one room, one teacher, and five grades of pupils. Lena was double-promoted right away because she was far advanced beyond the other children her age. She was pleased about this until she realized that the other children her age were jealous of her. Her good looks and fair skin also set her apart from the other children. They taunted her and made her feel "different." She realized that if she was to belong she would have to act more like the others and adjust herself to fit her current situation. She changed her way of speaking so that she sounded more like her classmates and less like a northerner, downplayed her superior learning, and dressed more like they did. After a time, the others began to accept her and stop taunting her.

But she also learned that for a Negro in the South there were some situations that one simply could not adjust to. One day Lena's mother called her into the house and dressed her up and announced that they were going to see a traveling tent and road show of black vaudeville performers. With a group of her mother's friends, they set off in a car for the show, which was in a neighboring town. Along the way, they were waved down and stopped by another carload of frantic black adults who warned them not to continue. In near hysteria, these people told Edna and her friends that to go ahead was to risk their lives. An angry mob of whites had lynched one of the black men in the tent show, they said. They did not know why the lynching had happened, but they did know that the white mob was prowling around looking for other black victims. Anything could happen in that atmosphere, and anyone among them could be the next target of white violence.

Lena saw the agonizing fear that overtook her mother and the other adults in the car when they heard the story of the killing. The looks on their faces, the strained, hushed tones of their voices, their sense of panic and helplessness caused Lena to be afraid, too. Although the adults did not tell Lena what was going on, she had heard enough, and even if she had heard nothing at all she could sense their fear. She knew that these people, who were grown-ups and thus supposed to be responsible for protecting her, were so afraid themselves that she could not count on their protection. Although they did turn around and head back to Miami, Lena would not forget the terror she had felt on that trip.

For Lena, life with her mother was a succession of upsetting, painful, and frightening situations—so many, one strung after the other, that later she could not distinguish among them. The only thing that was constant was their lack of money. Lena's mother could never seem to make enough money as an actress to pay for adequate food or clothing, or a decent place to stay. Edna Horne often wrote to her husband for help, but Teddy Horne steadfastly refused to send money as long as his wife insisted on keeping Lena with her.

So Lena and her mother lived from job to job. Work for Edna would turn up in some far-off place, and she would pack up and go, sometimes taking Lena with her, usually leaving her daughter in the care of strangers. Lena received more training in how to get along with all kinds of people, stay out of trouble, try to be accepted. But as hard as she tried, people almost always found her different, and after a time Lena began to stop trying to belong. Instead, she learned how to build a protective wall around herself, isolating herself from others so that she would not offend them and would not feel badly about not being one of them.

Fortunately, she did go back to Brooklyn for occasional visits, and she always felt relieved to be with people who knew her and with whom she belonged. But these visits served only to intensify Lena's growing desire for a stable home life and made returning to her mother even harder. Still, she continued to want to please her mother and to be with her mother. She felt protective toward the older woman, who wanted so much to be successful but who couldn't seem to manage it, and who seemed so high-strung that the least little problem upset her. Lena could not imagine how her mother would be able to get along alone.

When Edna Horne could find no more work in Florida, she and Lena spent a short time in Alabama. Edna's next acting job was in southern Ohio, and there Lena started to have terrible nightmares. Her mother was afraid to take her on the road in that condition, and so she left Lena in the care of a doctor's family. Although Lena felt welcome in the doctor's home, and was comforted by the doctor's spinster sister when she had nightmares, she could not seem to get rid of them. She would read late into the night, trying to avoid sleep and the bad dreams that accompanied it. She did not stop having nightmares until she and her mother went to Macon, Georgia, to live, and Lena had a chance to feel like part of a family again.

From Macon, Lena's mother went off to work in other cities and towns, and as usual she left her daughter in the care of strangers. By now, Lena was fairly used to moving into strange households, but even on the basis of her experience the household in Macon was unusual. She lived with a woman who was over ninety years old, the woman's daughter, and several great-grandchildren in a two-room house with an outdoor toilet that was shared with the neighbors. But the poorest family with whom Lena had ever lived also proved to be the most loving.

The women, especially the old one, were very kind to Lena. When she developed rickets, a disease of the bone caused by malnutrition, the old woman tenderly nursed her back to health with home remedies. When Lena's frail legs gave her pain, the woman wrapped them in brown bags soaked in vinegar, and the pain eased. The old woman also attacked the source of the problem by making sure Lena had big helpings at meals. The food—white cornmeal bread, biscuits, sweet potatoes cooked in the ashes of the fire, greens, and chicken with dumplings—was new to Lena, and she learned to love it.

The entire life-style of the family was new to Lena. The women made soap in a big iron pot in the front yard. The old woman dipped snuff—powdered tobacco that is placed between the lower lip and gums where the porous tissue allows the tobacco to seep into the bloodstream. At night, Lena and the other children climbed onto their cots around the old woman's bed and listened as she read from the Bible or told them biblical stories from memory.

One day, without warning, Lena's Uncle Frank appeared while she was playing in the front yard. Apparently, Lena's mother had contacted him and asked him to look after her. Uncle Frank, one of Lena's father's brothers, could not have had a very good impression when he came upon the little two-room house. He decided to take his niece away from that environment of poverty and did not pay much attention to whether or not she was loved there. So, Lena left the two good women and all the grandchildren and went to live in Fort Valley, Georgia.

Frank Horne was a college graduate. In fact, of Edwin and Cora Horne's four sons only Lena's father, Teddy, decided that college had nothing to teach him. Frank Horne was also a published poet and a trained optometrist, *and* would later be a member of President Franklin D. Roosevelt's "Black Cabinet," a group of black men who acted as his informal advisers on Negro affairs. But Frank Horne liked teaching best, and so he devoted most of his efforts to teaching at Fort Valley State College, a black college where the students were educated not only in academic and technical subjects but also in deportment.

Since her uncle was unmarried, Lena did not live with him at Fort Valley. Instead, she lived with her uncle's fiancée in the girls' dormitory at the college. She enjoyed being around the older girls, but she was constantly reminded that she was different. If she wasn't being told by the girls that she was too young to share in their conversations, then her uncle was admonishing her that she must have pride in herself. The older girls straightened their hair, and Lena wanted to do the same, but her uncle forbade it, pointing out that her hair was not so curly that it needed to be straightened.

At the nearby school she attended, the children her own age called her "yaller," a southern term for light-skinned. Some called her a bastard because she did not live with her parents.

Despite these problems, Lena remembers the two years she spent in Fort Valley with her Uncle Frank as among the happy times in her childhood. One reason was that her father visited her there. He spent over a month in Fort Valley, recuperating from a serious automobile accident, and Lena had the chance to spend more time with him then than she had since he'd left her and her mother in Brooklyn. Another reason was that she believed that her auburn-haired, blue-eyed uncle was the most beautiful and friendly man she had met since leaving her grandfather in Brooklyn. He was strict, but in a nice way, and since he was a blood relative Lena felt somehow secure. She later said of Fort Valley, "It was the one place I was often not afraid to be myself, because I did have one tie—my uncle." Thus, when her mother suddenly appeared to take her away, Lena did not want to go. But she had no choice.

Lena's mother and a girlfriend had bought a small house in Atlanta, Georgia, and this was Lena's next "home." Hardly had she settled in when her mother and the girlfriend, also an actress, were called away to work. Edna Horne hired a married couple to stay with Lena while she was away, and the wife turned out to be as cruel as the woman in Miami. The difference was that this woman wasn't able to use concern for Edna Horne's nerves as an excuse to beat Lena. Edna wasn't even there. This woman simply accused Lena of "wrongdoings," and every Wednesday and Saturday night, like clockwork, she punished Lena for them. She said she was making sure that Lena would not grow up to be like "show folk."

Lena tried to be on her best behavior and avoid the beatings, but she soon realized that there was no way to avoid them. When Lena did everything correctly, the woman still made it her business to find something she'd done that was punishable. She would tell Lena to dust a table, then put on a white glove and run her gloved hand over the table's surface. If she found so much as a particle of dust, she had her reason to beat Lena. She would order Lena to take a bath, then go outside and cut a switch from a nearby tree. Then, as Lena cowered wet and naked, the woman would lash her with the switch.

Although her mother came back to visit several times during this period, Lena never told her what happened. Finally, sympathetic neighbors who overheard Lena's cries of pain and humiliation told Edna Horne about the abuse of her daughter. Edna wept and asked Lena why she hadn't been the one to tell her that she had been receiving beatings. Lena never answered that question.

Edna Horne felt very guilty about what had happened to

Lena. Not long after she had rescued her daughter and fired the couple who had been responsible for taking care of her, she and her girlfriend could not meet the mortgage payments on the house and were forced to give it up. She now gave up trying to make a life for herself and her daughter. At last, she took Lena back to Brooklyn.

3

Lena Goes to Work

By the time Lena returned to live in the house on Chauncey Street, she was nearly fourteen years old, but she had lived in more places and met more strangers than most people twice her age. She had also suffered more mistreatment. She had been abused, both physically and psychologically. She had been exposed to terrifying and hateful things. And worst of all, she had suffered for nothing, because in the end she and her mother had not been able to stay together.

The Lena who returned to live with her grandparents was as well behaved as they remembered her to be, but she was more distant, more silent. Both Edwin and Cora Horne realized that their granddaughter had erected barriers around her heart, around her real thoughts and feelings, to protect herself from the constant flow of strange people and new places she had encountered and adjustments she had been forced to make during the years of roaming with her mother. Edwin Horne welcomed Lena back with his gentle ways, his books, and his classical-music records. Cora Horne hardly allowed Lena to unpack before she began criticizing Lena's mother for what had happened to Lena. Lena sprang to her mother's defense, and the two argued bitterly and incessantly. At times Lena wondered if returning to live with her grandparents had been such a good idea after all. Not for many years did she realize that by challenging her to speak up, and defend her mother, Cora Calhoun Horne was forcing her to break out of her shell.

Challenged by her grandmother, gently allowed to just "be" by her grandfather, and good-naturedly welcomed back by her Uncle Burke, Lena began to feel a real sense of security again. She renewed childhood friendships and made new friends as she adjusted to Girls' High School in Brooklyn. Although she had not lived in Brooklyn for many years, she found this latest adjustment comparatively easy. She had "ties," she had a last name that meant something to other people in the community. She began to dare to be herself.

A year after Lena returned to Brooklyn, her grandmother died of an attack of bronchial asthma. She'd suffered, and survived, many such attacks before, and no one in the family was prepared for her death. Least of all her husband. Edwin Horne and his wife had not enjoyed a happy marriage, but Lena believes that the couple shared a deep bond that no one else understood. It was the only way she was ever able to explain to herself why Edwin Horne just seemed to let go and die, too, a couple of months later. As an adult, she regretted not having had enough time with her grandparents to really have a chance to understand them.

Left alone in the house on Chauncey Street were Uncle Burke, who was in college, and young teenager Lena. Burke could manage by himself, but he was in no position to be responsible for his niece. Lena moved yet again, this time to the home of Mrs. Laura Rollock, a friend of the family. It was a perfect time for Lena to retreat into her shell, but fortunately Mrs. Rollock gave her no reason to do so. In fact, she encouraged Lena to continue to be herself and to be proud of who she was. Although Mrs. Rollock was respected in the community and active in the National Urban League and the National Association for the Advancement of Colored People, as Lena's grandmother had been, she differed from Cora Calhoun Horne in most other ways. She was a fine housekeeper, a good cook, and didn't think it was frivolous for a teenage girl to have friends over when she wanted to. Lena was happy in the Rollock home and relieved to be able to continue readjusting to the life she had known as a young child.

Then Lena got a letter from her mother telling her that while working in Cuba she had met and married Miguel Rodriguez, a white man. That made "Mike" her new father, and the newly-weds were returning to Brooklyn where Mike would take care of them and they would be a family again. Lena was stunned. She was comfortable in her new life with Mrs. Rollock. She did not want to go and live with her mother under any circumstances. Memories of the old miseries started to surface in Lena's mind, threatening to push her right back into her shell.

Just as she had promised in her letter, Lena's mother soon arrived with her new husband, full of plans to settle in Brooklyn. But the black middle-class people there deeply resented Edna's marriage to a white man and openly snubbed them. They moved to the Bronx, taking Lena with them.

Lena was angry and upset about being forced to leave her friends and her school. She did not like the Bronx high school where she had to enroll and was unable to make friends easily. She tried to keep in touch with her friends back in Brooklyn, but this was very difficult given the distance and the way the people in her old neighborhood felt about her mother's marriage. She was isolated among strangers again, and once again she also felt the terror of poverty.

Edna and Mike arrived in the United States from Cuba right in the middle of the Great Depression, a time when many Americans were unemployed, when thousands of people stood in lines to receive a bowl of soup from charity as their only meal of the day. In times like these, there was little work for the unskilled Edna. Mike was also unable to find work.

Lena remembers that Mike was in a constant state of fury. He was angry over not being able to find a job. He was angry and resentful over the racism of both whites and blacks in America. He couldn't understand why blacks did not try to fight discrimination and often made unkind and disparaging remarks about the black race. Mike's negative attitude and remarks about blacks caused Lena to suspect that although Mike cared for her and her mother, he did not really respect their race.

When Mike wasn't venting his fury against the poor job market or black people, he turned it on Lena, or so it seemed to her. Whenever she did anything to upset her mother—and her mother was very easily upset—Mike berated her. It was a situation that reminded her of the time she and her mother had lived in Florida. Again, she was being forced to put her mother's interests ahead of her own.

If either Mike or Edna had been able to find a job, the mood in the household might have improved, but neither could get work. The family was forced to turn to relief groups for food. They had to give up their apartment in the Bronx and move to a dirty tenement building in Harlem. The situation finally became so serious that Edna and Mike decided that Lena would have to go to work. For her part, Lena was more than willing to do so. She had never liked the school she attended in the Bronx, and liked it even less now that she had to commute there from Harlem. She was as eager as her mother and Mike to have some decent food and a better place to live. Besides, she hoped that bringing home some money would cause her mother and Mike to give her a little more respect.

Lena was sixteen by then. She had no real skills, but she had beauty. Tall and long-legged, with smooth, honey-colored skin and long black hair, she made heads turn when she walked down the street. Mrs. Rollock had paid for singing and dancing lessons for her, and so she knew the basics of performing. Her mother decided that this was enough to get Lena into show business. It was a world that Edna had always dreamed of conquering, but she had failed. She now began to hope that her daughter could fulfill those dreams. What's more, she had decided that her daughter was not going to spend years in cheap vaudeville houses while hoping for a break, as she had done. Her daughter was going to start at the top. Through a friend, she arranged for Lena to audition at the Cotton Club.

Located on the northeast corner of Lenox Avenue and 142d Street, the Cotton Club occupied a space that had been built as a dance hall in 1918. Owney Madden, a New York mobster, had bought it in 1923 and turned it into a nightclub that seated seven hundred people. Madden was not so much interested in operating a nightclub as he was in providing an outlet for the sale of his "Madden's Number 1" beer, which he made and sold illegally.

It was the time of Prohibition in the United States. Back in 1919, when Lena was only two years old, Congress had passed a law banning the manufacture and sale of all alcoholic beverages, unless they were used as medicine. From the start, it was a law that was impossible to enforce. The manufacture and sale of alcoholic beverages became the biggest illegal industry the country had ever known. It was during Prohibition that "organized crime" really got organized. The nightclub and saloon business also grew during Prohibition. The clubs hid their liquor supplies in secret rooms, and had alarm systems that warned when the police were coming so everyone could hide their liquor. But most of the time they just paid bribes to the police, so the authorities would look the other way.

Owney Madden opened up the Cotton Club in Harlem because it was also the time of the Harlem Renaissance, a period when blacks and their writing, music, and dancing were very popular among rich and sophisticated whites. These white people had first become interested in black musicals on Broadway which featured jazz singing and dancing. That interest had led them up to Harlem and the jazz clubs there. But they didn't want to mingle with blacks, they just wanted to watch them, and so clubs like the Cotton Club, even though they were right in the middle of Harlem, did not usually admit black patrons. As a rule, the only blacks in the Cotton Club were waiters and entertainers.

In the ten years since it had opened, the Cotton Club had become famous for its extravagant floor shows, its wealthy and important clientele, and its exclusive atmosphere. Everyone who was anyone in high society or political circles went there. The music played by the Cotton Club bands was broadcast live on radio, and black performers who appeared at the Cotton Club were almost guaranteed bookings anywhere else. Although black Americans did not like the idea that they could not patronize the Cotton Club, they were accustomed to segregation. What was more important to them was that black performers were getting a chance to become famous there.

Lena had heard people talk about the Cotton Club as far back as she could remember. While living with Mrs. Rollock, she had often listened to the broadcasts from the Cotton Club on the radio in her bedroom. The names of the Cotton Club bandleaders, like Duke Ellington and Cab Calloway, were magical to her, and when, in Brooklyn, she had had a chance to meet Cab Calloway at a charity function, she had been in awe of him. Thus, when her mother told her she had arranged for her to audition at the club, she was excited and eager to get the job.

As Lena recalls, no one who saw her audition was very excited about her talent, which she displayed by singing a couple of songs and dancing a couple of steps. She was hired mostly because she had the right "look." Cotton Club girls were young, tall, well-built, pretty, and light-skinned. A year earlier, Lucille Wilson, tall and beautiful but dark-skinned, had been hired on a trial basis and kept on, but she was the exception. She later married Louis Armstrong. The club management still believed that the important white clients preferred light-skinned chorus girls. Lena, at sixteen, was several years younger than the other girls, but the producers of the Cotton Club shows liked the idea and believed that the customers would like it, too. Lena joined the exclusive chorus line at the Cotton Club.

The black press kept careful track of such things as additions to the Cotton Club chorus line, and Lena's mother made sure all the papers knew about her daughter's being hired at the famous club. The story made headlines. Soon, a truant officer came to call, for Lena, at age sixteen, was not supposed to be staying away from school in order to work. Lena's mother explained that the family needed Lena's income in order to survive, and he understood. He agreed to report simply that Lena was "missing." Over in Brooklyn, Lena's former neighbors and friends of her grandmother were scandalized by the news that Lena had a job at the Cotton Club. Being a chorus girl was not considered respectable, particularly not in a whites-only club run by gangsters. They made sure both Lena and her mother knew how they felt.

Lena did not like being criticized, but she had lost touch with her friends in Brooklyn and had resigned herself to not going back to their world. Besides, she was too exhilarated about her chance to enter a new world that she thought would be exciting and glamorous. Her mother took the criticism from Brooklyn more seriously. She had not forgotten the reaction to her marrying a white man, and she had been embarrassed to be in such financial straits that she'd had to rely on charity for food. She determined that her daughter would work at the Cotton Club and earn money for the family, and still retain her virtue.

Lena's mother had accompanied her to the audition at the Cotton Club. Once Lena was hired, her mother continued to accompany her to the club nearly every night. She stayed backstage in the dressing room while Lena performed out front, and when the last show was over, escorted her home. None of the men at the club, either performers or patrons, could get past Edna. Even on the rare occasions when her mother was not with her, Lena was not approached by the men. She was under the legal age of consent—the term used then was "jail bait"—and they could have been arrested for propositioning her.

As if her age and the frequent presence of her mother were not enough, Lena also had protection from her father and his friends. Although Teddy Horne moved around a lot, he had many friends in Harlem's "sporting world." These gamblers and numbers runners did business with Owney Madden and his gang and were among the few blacks who were allowed admittance to the Cotton Club, although they generally sat near the kitchen. These men had known Lena since she was a baby, and they told her to let them know if anyone bothered her. When Teddy Horne learned that Lena was working at the Cotton Club, he began to make frequent visits to New York and the club. He, too, told her to let him know if she had any trouble.

Although Lena understood that her mother and her father and his friends meant well, at times she felt smothered by all that protection. Her mother seemed obsessed with preserving Lena's chastity and lectured her all the time about being "good." Lena was not at the Cotton Club long before she realized what a contradictory situation she was in. She was being a "good girl" and earning her family's primary income in a sexually charged environment. Sexual implications were integral to the shows.

The chorus girls' costumes were skimpy, and their movements were choreographed to entice. Lena heard talk that the older girls were sometimes expected to give more private entertainment to some of the white male customers. Although she was not asked to do so, she was expected to show off her body just like the others when she was in the line. Then she had to go backstage and listen to another lecture on virtue from her mother. But she listened to her mother, and stayed away from the men. She had little opportunity to meet boys.

Becoming a chorus girl at the age of sixteen cut Lena off from the normal life of a teenager. Having quit school, she no longer associated with young people her own age—certainly not the "respectable" young people her mother approved of. On the rare occasions when she was able to spend some time with her Brooklyn friends, Lena realized that she did not fit in with them anymore. While they were dating and partying she was working. While they were picnicking and going to movie matinees she was sleeping.

What made matters worse was that her mother would not let her associate with the adults in her new world. When she was hired at the club, the older chorus girls tried to be friendly and helpful, but Edna had rebuffed them. Naturally, they resented the idea that Lena was somehow special. After that, most of them ignored her. Once again, Lena was set apart, denied the chance to make friends among the people who surrounded her. She began to wonder if she would ever be allowed the simple privilege of belonging and despaired of having a family who, by insisting that she was special, made her feel like an outcast.

Thus, it meant a great deal to her that Cab Calloway and his band headlined her first Cotton Club show, and that Calloway actually recognized her. While living in Brooklyn, Lena had joined a group of teenage girls called the Junior Debs. They had served as hostesses at a charity ball for which Calloway and his band had played and had hung around the bandstand, excited to be near such famous musicians. When Cab Calloway saw Lena at the Cotton Club, he remembered her from Brooklyn. He called her "Brooklyn" and took her under his wing, giving her advice about how to make it in the Cotton Club revue, and in her new world. Even Edna could not object to Lena's being friendly with one of the stars of the show. For Lena's part, she cared more about having a friend than associating with a glamorous star.

For all its seeming glitter, the world of the entertainers at the Cotton Club was anything but glamorous. The working conditions were abominable; they would not be allowed today, and they were far worse than working conditions in the downtown clubs of that time where white performers worked. But there was so little work for black performers that the managers of the Cotton Club could treat them any way they wanted to. Brilliant talents like Calloway, Duke Ellington, Ethel Waters, Juano Hernandez, and Jimmie Lunceford worked for wages far below what white performers in downtown clubs were paid. They had tiny, poorly lit dressing rooms, no complimentary food or drinks, and no power to change these conditions.

If the headliners had to work under such poor conditions, life at the Cotton Club was much worse for a mere chorus girl. Lena and the others worked from eight-thirty at night to three in the morning, doing three shows a night, seven days a week. Between shows they crowded into a small, cramped room in back of the star's dressing room where they grabbed bits of Chinese food from paper containers, changed costumes, fixed their makeup, and tried not to have to go to the bathroom. There was only one ladies' room in the club and that was supposed to be reserved for the white customers.

The girls were paid twenty-five dollars a week, but their pay was docked if they were late, missed a show or a rehearsal for any reason, or broke any other rule. Yet they were often expected to work extra hours—performing downtown at vaudeville houses, at political functions, for important people, even once at Sing Sing prison in upstate New York—without receiving extra pay.

Still, at first Lena did not mind the bad working conditions, or the exploitation. She was working at the famous Cotton Club and she was earning some money. Most exciting for her was appearing on the same stage with the talented stars she had heard and read about. Although the Cotton Club was hardly a haven for black performers, it was a place where they could find work, and working was the important thing. They took the opportunity to do what they loved best and somehow managed to cope with the exploitation. They were dedicated to their art, and most of them overcame the various barriers set in their way and were highly successful. They contributed enormously to the American music tradition, and the exposure they received at the Cotton Club was important to all their careers.

By the time Lena Horne joined the Cotton Club girls, the club was well past its heyday. White interest in going up to Harlem to hear black jazz music and see black jazz dancing was on the wane; Prohibition was about to be repealed (it ended officially in December 1933); and gangster wars over the illegal businesses that were left made Harlem less safe for nighttime club-goers. The stock market had crashed in 1929 and the depression had quickly set in, and by 1933 the Harlem breadlines were hard for the white revelers to ignore. Also, some of the white revelers were beginning to watch their budgets and not spend as freely as before, because the effects of the depression were reaching the wealthy people, too. Although the Cotton Club management refused to relax the whites-only policy, or lower the cover charge, they did begin to cut back on the size of the lavish revues. Lena's second show at the club was the last big revue, and the last one written by the famous songwriting team of Harold Arlen and Ted Koehler.

It was in this show that Lena got her first featured spot. Arlen and Koehler had written a song called "As Long As I Live," and Avon Long, who ultimately became a famous dancer, and a female partner were to sing and dance to it. At practically the last moment, the girl who had been cast as Long's partner quit, and Lena got the chance to take her place.

Her mother was overjoyed. The stars in Edna's eyes burned even more brightly now. She was certain that stardom was just around the corner for her daughter, and she began to push the show's producers and the club's management to feature Lena even more. When they brushed her off, Mike got angry.

Since Lena had started working at the club, Mike had been there frequently, too, and every time he was present the tension backstage increased. He didn't think the "hoods" who ran the club treated Edna with enough respect. He criticized the black men who worked at the club for not standing up for their rights and protecting their women from the indignities they suffered there. For their part, the black men viewed Mike as an outsider who had not only stolen one of their women but also presumed to tell them how to treat the others. Sometimes Lena wondered if there would ever be an end to the arguing and bad feeling.

She was beginning to wonder, too, if there would ever be any letup in her exhausting work routine at the club. She worked seven nights a week until 3:00 A.M. She arrived home tired and weary and fell upon the living room sofa, where she tried to sleep until her mother and Mike got up, freeing the only bed in the apartment for her. Often, she would have to get up before she was fully rested in order to do special daytime performances arranged by the Cotton Club management. Although her salary of twenty-five dollars a week was respectable compared to the sixteen dollars for a stenographer and five to ten dollars for a salesclerk, it still was not enough to enable her family to move from the roach-infested Harlem tenement into a better apartment. Mike and the building superintendent worked hard to keep it clean, but it remained a source of shame for everyone in the family. If being a featured performer at the Cotton Club could not enable Lena to move her family to a decent home, then her career was not paying off the way she, or they, had hoped.

A few weeks after the spring 1934 *Cotton Club Parade* opened, Lena learned that a Broadway producer was interested in casting her for a part in his new show, *Dance with Your Gods*, starring Rex Ingram and Georgette Harvey. The part was a small one, described simply as "A Quadroon Girl," but it was still a chance to be on Broadway. Lena wanted it.

But she couldn't leave the Cotton Club. When Lena had been hired by the club, her mother had signed an iron-clad, lifetime contract that gave the club's management complete control over her work and barred her from working anywhere else. The producer of *Dance with Your Gods* had to get the Broadway mob to intercede with the Madden people and persuade them to let Lena work outside the club. By the terms of the deal that was finally struck, Lena would skip the first show at the club in order to perform in the Broadway show, then dash back uptown for the two later shows at the club.

Unfortunately, Lena's debut on Broadway was short-lived. The show was a flop and closed within two weeks. Lena had barely had time to become comfortable in her small role, much less learn to act, and there had been little chance for her to get the exposure on the Broadway stage that might have led to other stage roles. The director of the play told Lena that he could make an actress out of her if given more time, and this encouragement was enough to cause Lena's mother and Mike to try to get Lena out of the contract that gave the Cotton Club's management so much control over her career.

When the club bosses tried to stall on the matter of a new

contract, and tried to brush Mike off with false promises, the hot-tempered Cuban decided to force the issue, and to show the black men who worked at the club what they should have been doing all along. He confronted the Madden people and demanded that Lena's contract be revoked. In return, he was seriously beaten and his head stuffed down into a toilet bowl. The next day, one of the bosses told Lena that she had better remember who she was. She was not special to them; but still, she could not work anywhere else. For all her family's trouble, Lena got a five dollar a week raise.

4

Teenage Bride

*F*ournoy Miller was a performer-in-residence at the Cotton Club. A comedian, he had first become successful as part of the comedy team of Miller and Lyles. Back in 1921 he and Aubrey Lyles, together with the vaudeville music team of Noble Sissle and Eubie Blake, had written, directed, starred in, and produced *Shuffle Along*, the first black show to make it to Broadway and the show that is said to have started the Harlem Renaissance. Flournoy Miller thus had experience in producing shows. He was also a college graduate. But at the Cotton Club he was a comedian, and that was all. He deeply resented the system that exploited blacks and prevented them from succeeding, and angered by the club's treatment of Lena and her family, he determined to help them. He suggested that Edna and Mike contact Noble Sissle, who by now was a well-known bandleader. Noble Sissle had been the first man to put beautiful black women on the stage, Miller explained; perhaps he could help Lena.

Edna and Lena made a secret trip to Philadelphia to audition for Noble Sissle. Lena knew exactly one song for which the band had an arrangement: "Dinner For One, Please, James." She sang it and Noble Sissle hired her. At the time, she was so happy to get the job that it didn't occur to her to wonder why. Much later, she said, "When I think that really great singers like Ella Fitzgerald were singing with competing bands like Chick Webb's I don't see why Noble wanted me. I couldn't sing jazz and I couldn't sing blues. All I could do was carry a simple tune simply. Perhaps he just wanted to do a good turn for somebody."

Lena literally fled New York and the Madden mob to join the Noble Sissle Society Orchestra in Philadelphia. Her mother and Mike went with her. One reason was that Lena was not yet eighteen and her mother did not want her traveling alone. Another was that both Edna and Mike enjoyed being in the entertainment world, even if only on the fringes. But they were also afraid of what Owney Madden's people might do once they discovered Lena's absence, and they preferred not to wait around to find out.

When Lena and her family joined the Sissle orchestra in Philadelphia in 1935, the band was spending most of its time on the road, playing a few days or a week in a city before moving on to the next engagement somewhere else. Life on the road is never easy for entertainers, but in those days, for black people, it was especially grueling. Hotels and restaurants were segregated; often it was difficult even to find a place to eat or sleep. The group was forced to live in small rooming houses and cheap hotels in the black section of town, often far away from where they were performing. Mike Rodriguez, being white, was not really welcome in these rooming houses and hotels, but his presence was tolerated because he was with the band.

His presence was tolerated by the members of the orchestra because Noble Sissle understood and shared Edna's and Mike's protective attitude toward Lena. But tensions and strains soon developed because of Mike's stubborn insensitivity to the circumstances of being black in America.

After Philadelphia, the orchestra was scheduled to go to Boston, where they were to be the first black band to play at the Ritz-Carlton Hotel. Concerned that everything go right, and hoping to avoid any racial incidents, Sissle coached Lena on how to act like a lady so she would be treated like one and spoke with great bravado about the need to protect black womanhood. Mike listened and said nothing. When the orchestra arrived at the Ritz-Carlton, they were informed that they must enter and leave the hotel by the kitchen door. Black people were still not allowed in the hotel as guests, and the first black orchestra to play there were not to expect special treatment. The most ladylike behavior on Lena's part did not erase the fact that she was a Negro.

Mike blew up over the incident. But he did not direct his anger at the hotel management. Instead, he assailed Noble Sissle for not insisting that he and his group be allowed to use another door. In Boston, and elsewhere, he exhorted the members of the band to act more aggressively, reminding them of the indignities they were constantly forced to suffer. He didn't see why segregation should be accepted just because it had always been accepted before. He refused to understand the subtle, lifelong process of racism and how it molded people's lives. Sissle and his band, and Lena, resented Mike's lack of understanding. They knew that he could not possibly know what they felt or why they behaved the way they did without having shared their experiences as black people. He had no right to belittle them. Furthermore, he had no right to criticize Sissle and the others when the only reason he was with them was that he was getting a free ride on Lena's ticket, and by the grace of Noble Sissle. Since he would probably be around as long as Lena was with the band, they wished he would shut up and leave them to do what they had to do in peace.

Mike's presence, his scorn for the men in the band, and their open contempt for him, exacerbated the already miserable conditions of a long road tour. The group traveled from city to city by bus, and often slept on it rather than spend time trying to find a hotel or rooming house that would accept them. Meals were eaten on the run, and often the food was not very good. Lena, who'd had little vocal training and who was using techniques that strained her voice to its limits, realized that her voice was not something she could always rely on to work. No one had told her that it had to be cared for, like an instrument. She didn't know anything about taking care of her voice, and subjected to the hardships of the tour, it was often in trouble.

Still, there were enjoyable aspects to working with the Noble Sissle Society Orchestra. It was a very "respectable" group and was invited to play at private parties for wealthy whites. It was very popular with the black middle class, and when they arrived in a new city or town, they were met by representatives of the local NAACP and interviewed by the black press. Sometimes they were themselves entertained in the homes of black doctors and lawyers and other prominent members of the community. On these occasions, Lena sometimes met boys her own age, young men she might have enjoyed dating. But if the band's schedule did not prevent her from having many dates, the attitude of her mother and Mike did. Usually all she could hope to do was to sit in a corner, or out on the porch, and hold hands with a boy. On the rare occasions when she did have a date, her family made such a fuss that her fun was spoiled before it even began. Lena couldn't understand why they would not trust her to date and have fun like other young women her age. She began to suspect that they were afraid if she started dating she might meet someone she wanted to marry, and marriage would crush their hopes for her career. Accordingly, Lena began to dream of marriage. Marriage would give her independence from her over-protective parents; it would give her the stable home she had never enjoyed for longer than a couple of years at a time; and it would free her from the endless miles and the unrelenting grind of singing on the road tour.

When the Noble Sissle Society Orchestra headed for the Midwest, many changes were in store for both the group and Lena. Racism was more evident, and since there were smaller black populations in the cities, the band had even more difficulty finding accommodations. In Terre Haute, Indiana, they were forced to spend the night on the grounds of the Clyde Beatty Circus. Mike had one of his blowups over this sad state of affairs, and Noble Sissle, all his patience used up, finally asked him to leave the tour. Lena's mother was miserable. She did not want to be separated from the husband who had stayed with her and tried to protect her, but she could not bring herself to leave Lena. Mike went back to New York and Edna continued with the tour.

After they left Terre Haute, the band headed for Cincinnati, Ohio. On the way, Noble Sissle was injured in an auto accident and had to be hospitalized for two months. He feared losing the band's hard-earned engagements, not to mention the band members themselves, who certainly could not afford two months without pay. He knew that he had to come up with some gimmick that would keep the audiences interested in his band while he recovered. With Edna's wholehearted support, he decided that the best gimmick was to have Lena lead the band. Fortunately, all Lena had to do was strut around on stage waving a long baton and looking as if she was leading the band. The musicians, as always, followed the first saxophone. The music remained good and the press liked their performance. The band actually got additional publicity while it was being led by Lena, who went by the name "Helena" for the duration of her stint as bandleader.

They were still in Cincinnati on June 19, 1936, the night of the first Joe Louis–Max Schmeling fight. During the breaks in their show, they crowded around a radio and listened to the match. When Joe Louis was beaten so brutally, Lena and many of the men in the band wept openly. Her mother found this display of emotion disgusting and criticized Lena for being upset over some man she didn't even know. She thought Lena's mind ought to be on the show.

For Lena, as for so many other black people of the time, Joe Louis was a symbol, someone who belonged to them whether they knew him or not. He was one of them, representing the race proudly, and it hurt when that symbol of dignity and pride was beaten down. Lena might have been isolated and considered "different" most of her life, but when it came to Joe Louis, her reactions were in tune with those of the majority of other black people. Most took his defeat very personally, remembering the many times their hopes and dreams had been dashed against the bloody fist of white racism.

Lena's mother may have stuck to Lena like glue, but she was quite out of touch with the inner workings of her daughter's mind and heart. She did not understand what Lena was feeling. Lena's sense of racial pride had developed in a way that was different from her mother's. Also, her mother did not know that Lena had actually met Joe Louis. When she was still working at the Cotton Club, Teddy Horne had come and taken Lena on a visit to Pompton Lakes, New Jersey, where Joe Louis's training camp was located. She had not told her mother where she had gone with her father, suspecting that her mother would not have approved of her visiting a boxer's training camp.

Teddy Horne visited his daughter again in Cleveland, where the Sissle orchestra traveled after leaving Cincinnati. With a young friend named Louis Jones, he drove to Cleveland from

Pittsburgh, Pennsylvania, where he lived with his second wife and operated a hotel and gambling room, as well as numbers games. After their engagement in Cleveland, the Sissle orchestra was scheduled to have a few days off, and Lena wanted to spend them with her father. She persuaded her mother to agree to the plan, pointing out that it would free Edna to visit Mike. Thus, when the band broke up for their brief vacation, Lena, accompanied by one of the musicians, took a train to Pittsburgh, while Edna headed for New York.

During his daughter's stay in Pittsburgh, Teddy Horne saw to it that she had a real break from the drudgery of life on the road. He took her to nightclubs where she could be the one who was entertained, and introduced her proudly to his friends. Louis Jones often accompanied them, and the two young people were strongly attracted to one another. Although he liked to gamble and had met Teddy Horne playing cards, Louis Jones was much more "respectable" than the men Lena was used to being around. He was the son of a minister and a graduate of West Virginia State College, at that time an all-black school. He was polite and respectful. In Lena's eyes, he represented the "normal" world, and she quickly decided she wanted to marry him. Louis, for his part, thought Lena was beautiful and would make a perfect wife.

When her time in Pittsburgh came to an end, Lena went to New York to tell Edna and Mike that she was not going to return to the Noble Sissle Society Orchestra. Instead, she was going to go to Pittsburgh and marry Louis Jones. Edna was distraught over this news; she protested that Lena was throwing her career away. She pleaded with Noble Sissle to talk to Lena, but Lena did not want to hear that her place was in show business and would not listen to him. Then Edna tried to get her former husband to intervene. Teddy Horne was also against the romance, although he didn't say why. But he believed that Lena, at eighteen, was old enough to make her own decisions. He refused to interfere in his daughter's life.

Lena went back to Pittsburgh and continued her courtship with Louis Jones. A few weeks later they were married in the living room of her father's home. The bride, not yet nineteen years old, wore black. She thought it was a sophisticated color and appropriate for the ceremony that marked her passage into adulthood, and the freedom and privileges for which she had longed.

Louis Jones was nine years older than Lena, but he had not been able to save enough money to set up a home for himself and his bride. They moved into a room in the home of one of his brothers and told each other it was a temporary situation and that soon they would have their own house. Although he was a college graduate, Louis had learned that there were few jobs for him that were equal to his education and intelligence. Like legions of black men before him, he was forced to take a job that was far beneath his ability. He worked as a clerk in the county coroner's office.

Louis resented the barriers that racism had put before him, the slights he suffered every day because he was black. He looked to his young wife for comfort and relief from the strains of living in the white world, but Lena did not know how to ease his burdens. She was completely unprepared for the giving part of marriage. She had thought about marriage only in terms of what it could do for her, what Louis could do for her.

For that matter, Louis was equally unprepared. He wanted a traditional wife, someone to cook for him and care for him and bear his children. He also wanted a wife who was beautiful. But he did not consider a wife as someone to really share his life with.

At the time of her marriage, Lena did not know how to cook a meal. Her mother had purposely kept her away from kitchens, not wanting her daughter's good looks marred by kitchen work. Lena did not mind when Louis taught her how to cook the plain foods he liked. But she did mind Louis's attitude about what was woman's business and what was man's business.

Louis and his brothers were ardent workers for the Democratic Party. In fact, it was through his work for the party that he had gotten his job in the county coroner's office. His party activities kept him away from home many nights, and Lena resented being left alone. She also resented his refusal even to talk with her about what he was doing. When party meetings were held in their home, he expected Lena to serve refreshments but not to sit in on the discussions. Remembering the activism of her grand-mother and Mrs. Rollock, Lena saw no reason why she should be excluded from her husband's activities, and they argued about it.

Louis also considered their financial affairs to be his business alone and would not talk to Lena about them. But Lena knew that they were in trouble when bill collectors began to hound them. She realized that her husband seemed to have no problem letting her deal with the bill collectors.

Fortunately, Teddy Horne was generous with monetary gifts, and Louis's family were affectionate and supportive toward Lena. With help from their families, Lena and Louis tried to adjust to the realities of marriage. Lena became pregnant and everyone looked forward to the arrival of the couple's first child.

During her pregnancy, Lena was attended by a black doctor, and when she went into labor in December 1937 she expected that the same doctor would deliver her baby. But when she and Louis arrived at the hospital, the doctor was waiting outside to tell her that the all-white hospital staff would take over at that point. Black doctors were not allowed to practice in that hospital. He thought Lena knew that.

Lena hadn't known, and she was terrified to give birth to her baby without her own doctor. Finding herself among complete strangers, she froze and was in labor for two days. After Gail was born at last, Lena and her infant daughter were segregated on a little ward reserved for black mothers, away from the white patients. She was not prepared for white middle-class racism. She was unhappy and upset and anxious to be discharged from that unfriendly hospital.

Soon after Gail's birth, Lena and Louis moved into their first home. Louis's sister came to help Lena with the new baby. The two had become good friends, and they enjoyed sharing Gail's care. Lena was happy to have the company, for Louis continued to spend many evenings at political meetings. Then, when Gail was just four months old, Lena was offered a chance to resume a career of her own—in Hollywood.

Harold Gumm, a movie agent, called from New York to offer her a part in a Hollywood film, and Lena was excited about the prospect of doing a movie. But she was concerned about leaving her baby so soon. She and Louis talked the matter over and decided that the money Lena could earn would ease their financial predicament, which was even more serious now that they had a baby and a house. So, wearing the new outfit that Louis thought she ought to have, but for which they went into further debt, Lena left Gail in the care of her sister-in-law and set off for Hollywood.

5

Back in Show Business

The movie for which Lena had been hired was called *The Duke Is Tops*, and it starred Duke Ellington and his orchestra. Lena was cast as Ralph Cooper's wife in a story about a husband and wife who are both in show business and whose marriage is threatened by their two careers. It was a "quickie musical," scheduled to be shot in just a few weeks, and Lena was expected to go to work as soon as she reached Hollywood. Although filming soon began, she did not get paid. The producers had not been able to raise the money they had promised to pay the actors and actresses. The members of the cast were naturally upset about not being paid, but they decided to stay with the picture. The producers had promised to raise the money for their salaries, and there was so little work in Hollywood for black actors and actresses that Lena and the others decided it was better to work for the promise of pay than not to work at all.

But when Lena called home and told Louis the situation, he demanded that she come home at once. He didn't want his wife working without pay. Lena explained to Louis that if she walked out on the picture, her action might throw all of the other people in the film out of work. She told him that to do such a thing would violate a long-standing, unwritten rule among theater people: Never walk out on a show. She would jeopardize her professional standing if she did. Louis did not understand, but when he was unable to persuade Lena to change her mind he started calling Harold Gumm in New York, and demanding Lena's money.

Although *The Duke Is Tops* was completed, Lena never did receive the full salary that had been promised her. Louis was furious over the whole matter. When the picture premiered in Pittsburgh, the local chapter of the NAACP held a special benefit showing, and because Lena, a "hometown girl," was in the cast, she was invited as an honored guest. But Louis refused to allow her to attend.

Lena was beginning to feel that by getting married to Louis she had simply exchanged one kind of trap for another. Louis controlled her life nearly as much as her mother had, and that was not Lena's idea of the way she wanted to live. But she had a baby and responsibilities and gave no serious thought to leaving her husband.

Not long after the movie fiasco, in the fall of 1938, Harold Gumm called Lena again. This time he was offering her a part in Lew Leslie's *Blackbirds of 1939*, a Broadway show. Lew Leslie was one of the pioneers of the all-black show. Several of his *Blackbirds* revues had been hits and he had lined up an all-star cast for this one. Harold Gumm believed that Lena belonged in it, too.

After all of the trouble they'd had over the movie, Lena expected Louis to forbid her to participate in the show. Gail was not yet a year old, and Lena did not want to leave the family again. But to Lena's surprise Louis agreed and went ahead to work out business terms with Gumm. Soon, Lena, Gail, and a family friend who would babysit while Lena rehearsed, were on their way to New York.

Lew Leslie, Lena's new boss, had been producer for Florence Mills, a famous black singer of the 1920s whose records Lena's grandfather had played for her when she was a little girl. Florence Mills had died of acute appendicitis in 1927, and no one had mourned her passing more than Lew Leslie. He talked about her all the time. Her voice, he said, was high, sweet, and pure. She was a tiny woman with skinny legs and a stage manner that he described as "tender." Lena soon realized that Leslie wanted her to be like Florence Mills, and although in her opinion the only thing she had in common with the late star was skinny legs, she tried. But her voice was not high and pure, and working with Noble Sissle's orchestra had caused her to develop an aggressive stage manner. Eventually, Lew Leslie accepted the fact that she could not be another Florence Mills.

Once he had done so, he urged Lena to work hard to develop her own talent and stage manner. Lena listened and learned, and the two became close friends. This was Lena's first experience working with a boss who did not act like a boss. Lew introduced her to his family, and she enjoyed being in the warm atmosphere of a traditional and close Jewish family. Lena often joined Lew, his wife, and his brother for dinner after rehearsals at a favorite restaurant on the Lower East Side of Manhattan. She learned to enjoy Jewish cooking, and she learned for the first time that there were white people who were not prejudiced against Negroes.

Although Lew was very kind to Lena, he was experiencing financial problems, and once again Lena was not getting paid her full salary. While he didn't have enough money to pay his performers adequately, Leslie did make certain that they had rent and food money, but that wasn't enough to mollify Lena's husband. He was furious to learn that Lena wasn't getting paid, and he insisted that she come home immediately.

This time, Lena's response was defined by something more than her stubborn determination not to be unprofessional. Under

Lew Leslie's wise tutelage, she was learning that when she failed or succeeded she did so for no one but herself. She did not do it for her mother or Louis or Lew Leslie, or for any of the people that she had spent her entire life trying to please. While working in the *Blackbirds* show, Lena felt for the first time that she was a strong person capable of coping with her responsibilities. These new feelings of self-confidence enabled her to quietly reject Louis's demands that she quit the show.

After a lot of hard work and worry over money, the *Blackbirds* company was finally ready for a tryout in Boston. The show received lukewarm reviews there, and the entire company went into a panic. Without excellent reviews in Boston, Lew might not be able to raise the additional money needed to open the show in New York. In fact, he did not manage to raise the necessary money until just a few hours before curtain time. It was a tense few days. But instead of causing cast and producer to blame one another, the mutual anxiety served to draw them together. Everyone in the company liked Lew; they felt as if they were a great big family. Lena liked this feeling of closeness, of being part of a community effort. When the show did indeed open, she felt exhilarated.

Louis came from Pittsburgh for the opening, and Lena hoped he would go to the cast party with her afterward. That the show had opened at all was a wonder, and everyone involved had a real reason to celebrate. But Louis would have no part of the celebration, and he refused even to let her go. After that first night, there was little cause for further celebration by the *Blackbirds* cast. The show closed after only eight nights, and Lena, Gail, and the babysitter returned to Pittsburgh.

Lena returned home determined to end her marriage. She was furious with Louis for not letting her go to the opening-night cast party and tired of his refusal to understand the vagaries of show business. He thought she was a fool for appearing in a show that had flopped. She was tired of his criticism and his attempts to control her life. She went to her father for help, asking that she be allowed to stay with him for a few days to collect her thoughts and decide what to do.

But this time Teddy Horne refused to help his daughter; he wanted no part in the breakup of her marriage. Seeing how desperate she was, he decided to enlist the help of Louis's family. He arranged a family meeting. Lena's father, Louis's father and Louis's sister, who, according to Lena, was angry with Louis nearly as often as she was, all got together with the couple to help them try to iron out the problems in their marriage. They reminded the couple that they were both to blame for their problems and that they were both young and had a lot to learn. There was Gail to consider, and no one knew better than Lena how hard it was on a young child when his or her parents separated. At last, Lena and Louis bowed to family pressure and agreed to try to save their marriage. But neither really meant to try. Lena gave in because she had no one to help her. Her mother and Mike had gone to live in Cuba, and her father was firm in his decision not to let her stay with him. Louis had not changed his attitude about show business or about what a "woman's place" should be in a marriage. But both tried to go through the motions of making their marriage work.

Not long after the family meeting, Lena became pregnant again. She took no chances this time; she would not be deserted at the delivery room door. She hired a white doctor, and the birth of her son was much easier for her than her first delivery. She named the baby Teddy, after her father. Louis was proud to have a son, and the first male grandchild in the Jones family. In fact, he felt so possessive that he warned Lena that if she ever thought again about leaving him, "You are not going to get this boy. I'm going to take this boy from you." Lena was stunned by this threat, and more convinced than ever that the marriage could not work. But she tried to put this thought far back in her mind and concentrate on caring for her children.

In addition to his Democratic party activities, Louis belonged to a bridge club. Lena's mother had despised gambling or card-playing of any kind, and had deliberately kept Lena away from card games, so Lena did not know how to play. But she accompanied Louis to his bridge club games because he wanted her to. The other members of the bridge club were well-to-do, middle-class people, and Lena resented the money that Louis lost to people who had so much more than they. One of the other members of the bridge club was a woman named Charlotte Catlin. She liked Lena and made a point of being nice to her and making her feel included even though she only watched Louis play. Charlotte played the piano at parties in the most fashion-able white homes in the area, and knowing that Lena was a singer she eventually asked her to come along and sing at these parties. Lena had withdrawn into herself by now and lost all the self-confidence she had acquired while with Lew Leslie. She told Charlotte that she didn't have the nerve to ask Louis. So Charlotte asked him herself, explaining to him that the people who attended those parties were wealthy white socialites and that they paid well. Impressed, Louis agreed to let Lena sing with Charlotte.

Lena was glad to make the money to help out with groceries, and especially grateful that the small income would free her from having to ask Louis for money for the little items that she needed. She liked the work, and found the people quite charming. The experience was a good one for her, because it brought her out of her shell a bit. She was good with a lyric—she could get right to the heart of it—and Charlotte was an able teacher who helped Lena to improve her singing ability.

Meanwhile, Lena's relationship with her husband was not

improving, and when she saw that she was unconsciously communicating her tension to Gail she realized that eventually she would have to leave. As her own parents had been, she and Louis were badly mismatched. Although she was nine years younger than her husband, she was far more worldly in many ways. She had experienced night life as few other young women had, and she had seen strong women making it on their own in a man's world. Louis had spent his life in tradition-bound Pittsburgh. He knew nothing of the way of life Lena had led. He never managed to see Lena as a person; as his wife, she was more like his possession. Their ideas about the world and about marriage were radically different, and Lena was certain that there was no compromise possible.

Although singing with Charlotte Catlin had caused her to gain a little more self-confidence, Lena was still not ready to be on her own. But she decided to make plans for the time when she did get the courage to go. She asked her stepmother for a loan. While she and her father's second wife were not close, they did have a mutual respect for one another. Since she knew her father would do nothing to help her break away from her marriage, she approached her father's wife, explaining that she wanted to have enough money to escape to New York, if and when such a flight became necessary. The woman promised to give her the money when she needed it.

Assured of this help, Lena began to stand up to her husband and to voice her feelings more readily. One day while Louis was preparing to go on a political trip around the state, Lena discovered a box behind the living room sofa. In it was a pair of brand-new, handmade men's shoes. Lena, who had just finished putting off an angry bill collector, was furious. She confronted her husband, telling him that she was tired of the secretive way he handled their money and of such selfish extravagances as handmade shoes for himself. She told him she was leaving.

Louis did not take her threat very seriously. He told her that if she did leave, she would come back, just as she had the last time. He went off on his trip, taking his new shoes with him.

As soon as he left, Lena got busy. She collected the loan money from her stepmother, arranged for Teddy's babysitter, Mrs. Turner, to move in, and informed Louis upon his return that she was all set to go. He still did not take her seriously and belittled her ability to make it on her own. He told her that it was one thing to make it among Pittsburgh socialites, referring to the parties where Lena sang, and quite another to make it on her own. At this point, Lena lost all control. Her angry outburst was unlike anything Louis had seen from her before. She spat out all of the resentment and grievances and disenchantments that had accumulated over the years they had been together. Louis was shocked and could not understand how Lena could have held so much bitterness in for so long. Maybe if she had spoken up this way before, things might have been different. But Lena had learned to keep her hurt and misery inside, protecting the people around her from it. Finally the dam had burst and the years of anguish had poured out, and now she no longer cared what he thought.

Within two days of her uncharacteristic outburst, Lena left Pittsburgh for New York. Before she left, Louis reminded her that she would never get baby Teddy. Lena ignored this threat and left Teddy and Gail in Mrs. Turner's care, planning to return for them when she got settled and found work. She believed that the children belonged with their mother.

6
On Her Own

When she had first started working in New York, Lena had enjoyed the protection of her mother, and of her father and his friends. If anything, she had been overprotected. But when she arrived in New York late in 1939, she was entirely on her own and faced with the task of building a new life not just for herself but for her children. She prayed that her stepmother's money would last until she could find a job.

Lena checked into the Theresa Hotel in Harlem. The large gray building on Lenox Avenue and 125th Street was a fine hotel where black people could stay when hotels downtown refused to admit them. Many prominent black people have stayed there, and it was a hub of activity in the life of Harlem during that time. Years later, the hotel would draw national attention when Cuban premier Fidel Castro stayed there while on a visit to the United Nations: His entourage included live, caged chickens. By then it was no longer a luxury hotel and was soon turned into an office building. But in 1939, when Lena stayed there, it was still a most fashionable place.

When Lena walked through the lobby, the sporting-life men gave her a lot of attention, making sure that she knew of their interest in her as a woman. This interest bolstered Lena's shaken ego and inspired her confidence. She was not, after all, as defective as Louis had made her feel. Perhaps she would be able to find work quickly.

As soon as she had settled into the hotel, Lena began her job search. Just around the corner from the Theresa Hotel was the famous Apollo Theater where all the great black entertainers appeared, people like Duke Ellington, Ella Fitzgerald, Billie Holiday, Lionel Hampton, and Jay McShann, the man who had brought Charlie "Yardbird" Parker, the legendary musician and composer, to town. Lena had heard that Noble Sissle was in New York and she hoped she might find him there. But Noble was out of town and there was no work for her in the Apollo's chorus line, which she was secretly relieved to hear since she really didn't want to go back to "hoofing."

Next, Lena called Harold Gumm, the New York agent who had gotten her the role in *The Duke Is Tops* and the part in Lew Leslie's *Blackbirds*. Gumm invited her downtown to his office, where she had never been alone before. She gathered up her courage and tried to appear confident during their meeting. Gumm agreed to try to find work for her, but that proved very difficult. Racial stereotyping was very strong, and Lena just didn't fit the commonly accepted image of a Negro. Her skin was too light, her hair was too straight, her features too aquiline. Besides, she didn't sing the blues. One after another, white producers told her and her agent that she just wasn't the right type. One producer, George White, even suggested that she pass herself off as Spanish. If she did, he said, he would hire her.

Lena was surprised and angered by this suggestion. She became even angrier when her agent, who was as discouraged as she was about all the rejections, actually suggested that she consider George White's offer. There were plenty of people in her family who could pass as Spanish, or even white, but none of them had ever done so. Neither would Lena. It would be degrading for her and insulting to her family. Furthermore, if being Spanish was to be anything at áll like Mike, her mother's Cuban husband, she wanted no part of it.

Smarting from her defeat downtown, Lena went back to Harlem determined to renew her search for work there. Soon, she was invited to sing for a benefit show at the Apollo. The Noble Sissle orchestra was scheduled to appear on the same bill, and Lena approached Sissle about getting her old job back. Perhaps remembering how she had left him to get married, he told her that he did not have a job for her with his band, and she tried her best to hide her disappointment.

When Lena sang at the benefit show she wore a dress that her stepmother had sent her from Pittsburgh; she could not afford to buy clothes herself. She sang a Dinah Shore hit and a number from the Cotton Club act and another from the Betty Grable movie *Down Argentine Way*. She recalls that she was well received, but this small success was not nearly enough to lift her spirits. The next day, Lena started to feel depressed and fearful. She just did not know what the future held for her. How would she ever be able to take care of herself and her children? What was this madness all about that she was not black enough to be herself? Tired of looking at the four walls of her hotel room, she went by herself to the Victoria Theatre on West 116th Street. As she sat dejectedly, staring up at the screen, she heard a voice speak her name. It was Clarence Robinson, a dancer and choreographer at the Apollo. He had been looking for her to tell her about an opening in Charlie Barnet's band, an all-white band that was appearing at the Windsor Theater in the Bronx. One of the regular singers was sick and Barnet needed a replacement, fast. He'd called Robinson and Robinson had immediately thought of Lena. At first, Lena did not like the idea of appearing with an all-white band, but Robinson assured her that Barnet was a nice man and that Lena would have no difficulty working with him.

Lena got the job with Charlie Barnet, and within a few hours of her audition she was on stage performing. After the performance she called her stepmother in Pittsburgh because she wanted to know how her father would react to her working with an all-white band. Since her family was prejudiced against white people, her stepmother felt that he would object. Lena explained that it was the only job she could get, that she needed the work badly, and her stepmother encouraged her to keep the job. Lena was pleased to hear this and promised to start paying the loan back as soon as she drew her first check.

Now that she had a job, Lena felt that she could really begin to make plans for her new life with her children. Wanting to save money, and to pay back the money she owed, she moved out of the Theresa Hotel and into a room at the Harlem YWCA on 135th Street between 7th and Lenox Avenues. When she wasn't working, she spent most of her time in that room, listening to the radio. It was a good way to keep up with the latest music. Her favorite recording was "Stardust" by Artie Shaw, and she often called the disc jockey at the local radio station and asked him to play it for her.

Within a week of her hiring, Lena went on the road with Charlie Barnet and his band. It was the first time she had gone on a road tour without her mother. While some of the men in the band made passes at her, they did not show prejudice against her because she was black. She grew to like Barnet very much. He was independently wealthy and played music for the sheer joy of it, which earned him the respect of black audiences as well as white ones. He had managed to impress the musically sophisticated and highly critical audiences at the Apollo Theater, no small feat. Along with Artie Shaw, a white band leader whose lead female singer was Billie Holiday, Barnet was a pioneer in introducing black female singers to white audiences.

Barnet helped Lena artistically. Instead of asking her to sing standard arrangements, as she had always done before, he had songs specially arranged to suit her voice—to emphasize her strengths and at the same time to force her to improve upon her weaknesses. It was the first time that anyone had concentrated on her voice as an instrument, and the quality of her voice and singing improved while she was with Barnet and his band. She even did a recording with them—"Good for Nothing Joe."

Although Lena did not feel strange as a black woman with an all-white band, the fact that she was black did create some problems on the road. Hotels that were willing to accommodate Barnet and his musicians were not willing to admit Lena, and many times the men refused to stay in such hotels. Some of the colleges where they played refused to have a black singer perform; Lena would be given the night off, with pay. At other places, it was all right if she sang with the band, but there were objections if she sat on stage between numbers "mixing" with the white men. On such occasions, Lena would wait on the bus or in the "powder room" until it was time for her numbers. When she waited on the bus, some of the guys from the band would keep her company. But the bus was not always parked close by, and sometimes it was necessary for her to wait inside. Sitting alone in those restrooms, Lena developed a prejudice against white middle-class women that would last for years afterward. She resented the fact that she had to hide away in a toilet to protect their virtue. She was hurt that no one seemed to care how all of this made her feel, what sacrifices she had to make to preserve the aura of whiteness. Although Lena says that she can set this prejudice aside now, she is still leery of attractive white women.

When the time approached for the band to go to the South,

Charlie Barnet explained to Lena that he couldn't safely tour that region with a black singer; it was just too risky. But he did pay her for the entire period. Lena spent her time off with her stepmother on a steamboat cruise down the Mississippi to New Orleans, and while on that cruise she decided to quit the band. Although she liked Charlie Barnet and felt she had learned a lot during the six months she had been with him, she was tired of the difficulties and indignities of traveling with a white band. Besides, she had saved enough money to send for her children and make a home for them in New York.

Lena went to Chicago to visit her cousin Edwina and persuaded the woman to go to New York to live with her and care for the children. Once she had gotten her cousin's consent, she returned to New York and arranged to rent the Horne family home on Chauncey Street from her father. Then, she went to Pittsburgh to get Gail and Teddy. But there Louis carried out the threat he had made when Teddy was just an infant; he refused to let Lena take her son. Lena returned to Brooklyn with Gail only and tried to push away the guilt she felt over abandoning her little boy.

Although she grieved over not having Teddy with her, Lena felt a great sense of accomplishment once she had gotten Edwina and Gail settled in Brooklyn. She had managed to make a home for herself and her children, and she fully intended to have Teddy with her eventually. She felt like a responsible mother, and she enjoyed being the provider for the household. For the first time in her life she felt really in control of her life.

Now that she had the responsibility of a family, Lena moved quickly to get work in the New York show business world. Having promised to appear with the Barnet band when they returned to New York for an engagement at the Paramount Theater, she reaped the benefit of having immediate New York exposure; and it did not hurt her career at all to appear on the same bill with the popular white singer, Dinah Shore. By this time, "Good for Nothing Joe," which she had recorded with the Barnet group, had become a hit, and this, too, caused people to pay attention to her.

John Hammond had worked on the recording of "Good for Nothing Joe." A talented musician himself, Hammond had also proved talented in the management aspect of the music business. He had managed band leader Count Basie's first tour and brought Basie and singer Billie Holiday together. Respected by both blacks and whites, he was another pioneer in bringing black show business and white show business together. Before the 1940s, black and white show business had existed as separate, segregated, and unequal. Like Charlie Barnet and Artie Shaw, John Hammond was instrumental in creating a truly American form of entertainment that largely disregarded race, at least on the stage. He introduced Lena to yet another pioneer, Barney Josephson, who owned and operated a pair of nightclubs, Café Society Uptown and Café Society Downtown. Josephson was the first important white club owner to hire black entertainers and to have an integrated admissions policy. He also showed a great sensitivity to the elements of subtle racism.

When Lena auditioned for Barney Josephson, she chose to sing the song "Sleepy Time Down South." She had not sung more than a few bars when Josephson interrupted her and asked if she realized the implications of that song for her, a Negro. Lena was puzzled by the question; it was just a song, and since it was a currently popular song she had thought it would be a good one to sing at the audition. But Josephson pointed out that behind the idyllic image that the South liked to present, and that was presented in the song, was a system of cruel racism that caused untold misery and suffering to southern blacks. He said it was Lena's responsibility as a black person not to assist in maintaining myths that misled both blacks and whites about life in the South. He asked her to compare the lyrics of the song to the realities of southern black life.

Startled, Lena realized that Josephson was right, and to this day she has an aversion to that song. She was amazed and somewhat ashamed that a white intellectual had something to teach her about racism and her responsibilities as a black person. But she was not defensive. She sang "The Man I Love" and got the job.

Lena and Barney became friends, and he continued to teach her about herself as a black person. Like her stepfather, Mike, Barney Josephson was white and could never experience what it was like to be black. But unlike Mike he was intelligent and sensitive enough to understand racism and how it affected both blacks and whites. He helped Lena understand her negative feelings toward whites, how the country's centuries-old racial antagonisms influenced her actions and attitudes as well as those of other people.

He also helped her to understand better the music of her own people. Lena had been brought up by middle-class black people who did not like the blues, which they looked down on as low-class music. Thus, when Barney Josephson said he wanted her to sing some of Billie Holiday's songs at Café Society Downtown, Lena protested that she did not "feel" the blues. Barney insisted, and the patrons of the club enjoyed the satire of a black woman trying, but not knowing how, to sing the blues. Meanwhile, seeing Lena's discomfort, Barney talked to her about how blues music came about. He explained that it was a natural outgrowth of racism. He talked about the way black people had translated their misery into wonderful music.

For Lena, working for Barney Josephson was like going to school. In fact it was better, for even if she had finished high school and gone on to college she probably would not have learned what he taught her. In those days schools did not teach black history, and most blacks did not talk about slavery and the history of racism, even among themselves. Those few who did were considered extremely radical, or highly intellectual, or both. Under the influence of Barney Josephson, Lena learned to appreciate a great many things about black people, including their music, the blues.

At Café Society Downtown, Lena met and came to know many famous and talented people, among them folk singer Josh White, pianist Hazel Scott, and blues singer Billie Holiday. She became especially close to Paul Robeson, who had been a college athlete and a lawyer before going on to become famous as a singer and an actor. Robeson had known Lena's grandmother; in fact, Cora Calhoun Horne had helped Paul win a scholarship to Rutgers University in New Jersey. Paul had idolized Cora Horne. He shared with Lena his childhood memory of watching her grandmother confront a Harlem street gang and tell them how to spend their time properly. Paul Robeson had been raised in the black middle class, too, but he had not needed someone like Barney Josephson to tell him about being black. He had found out by himself, and he shared what he had learned with Lena. "You are a Negro," he told her, "and that is the whole basis of what you are and what you will become. When you live and learn some more you will be Lena Horne, Negro." Twenty-three-year-old Lena listened, and determined to understand.

From listening to the lyrics of Josh White's folk songs, Lena learned more about the social and moral aspects of racism. Being around pianist Hazel Scott exposed her to fierce racial pride. She and Hazel did not get along very well, but Lena had to admire Hazel's West Indian dignity. Billie Holiday was very kind and protective toward Lena; she did not mind when Lena sang her songs, like "Fine and Mellow," and in fact she complimented Lena on her singing. But no one could sing the blues like Billie Holiday, and Lena knew that. Billie was pure sadness and so vulnerable that Lena felt tough by comparison.

Through her association with these people and others, Lena felt stimulated, both intellectually and artistically. Her professional life was wonderful. Her private life was happy, too. Her Uncle Frank was living and working in Washington, D.C., where he was one of President Franklin D. Roosevelt's informal advisers, and visited her often. Her Uncle Burke was now manager at the Apollo Theater, and she saw a great deal of him. When Louis suddenly decided to let Teddy visit her, Lena felt as if life could not be better.

Although she had known that Teddy was only visiting and was not with her to stay, Lena grieved when Louis came and took him back to Pittsburgh. The departure of her son left a big hole in her life and caused her to question how happy she was with the rest of it. Thus, when Harold Gumm approached her with the chance to work in a new Hollywood club, she listened carefully.

The Club Trocadero, to be operated by a man named Felix Young, was to be a really high-class club with only the best black entertainers. Duke Ellington, Ethel Waters, and the Katherine Dunham dancers were already lined up to star there. Harold Gumm felt that working at the club would be a wonderful chance for Lena; she would get Hollywood exposure, and that would surely lead to movie roles.

Lena wasn't sure. Despite the "education" she had received from Barney Josephson, she still wasn't very comfortable around ordinary white people. She felt okay around the white people at Café Society Downtown, which was located in liberal Greenwich Village, but she didn't like it when occasionally she had to go up to midtown Manhattan and substitute for Hazel Scott at Café Society Uptown. Hollywood was not only a white town, it was also a racist town. Lena didn't know if she could handle living there, and some of her friends, among them Barney Josephson, didn't think she should even try.

But she had other friends who urged her to go. One of them was Walter White. He was national president of the NAACP and like Paul Robeson, who had introduced them, a friend of Cora Calhoun Horne's. Walter White was all for Lena's going to Hollywood to work. He felt that the Hollywood image of black people needed the dignity that Lena could bring to it. He was bitterly opposed to the prevailing stereotypes that blacks in Hollywood were forced to play—savages or maids and other servant types. Walter argued that Lena was strong enough to be exposed in Hollywood in a way that would combat the established tradition. He wanted to use Lena to break through the Tarzan-movie and servant images that blacks were trapped in out in Hollywood. He urged Lena to regard going to Hollywood as something bigger than her personal career. He wanted her to understand that it was an opportunity for her to be a pioneer, and he had great confidence in her ability to do so.

Although Lena stalled a while longer, she was deeply moved by Walter White's arguments. Barney Josephson and others had taught her about the history of racism. Now she had the opportunity to affect that history. She decided to go to Hollywood. When she announced her decision, Barney Josephson was so certain she was making a mistake that he stopped speaking to her. Lena resigned herself to the idea that losing Barney's friendship was one of the prices she had to pay for being a pioneer. She packed up Cousin Edwina and Gail and headed for the West Coast.

Chorus line of the Cotton Club, early 1930s. Lena Horne is fourth from right.

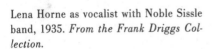

Lena Horne as vocalist with Noble Sissle band, 1935. *From the Frank Driggs Collection.*

(Right) Lena Horne and Noble Sissle, mid-1930s. *Photo courtesy of Duncan P. Schiedt.*

(Below) With Ralph Cooper in *Bronze Venus*, 1938. *From the Frank Driggs Collection.*

(Above) On "Chamber Music Society of Lower Basin Street," NBC Radio, c. 1940. *From the Frank Driggs Collection.*

(Bottom right) At Café Society. Count Basie, with cigarette in hand, stands behind Pete Johnson, the pianist. 1941. *From the Frank Driggs Collection.*

(Right) At Greenwood Lake, New Jersey, September 15, 1941. *Theatre Collection, Museum of the City of New York.*

With Eddie "Rochester" Anderson in *Cabin in the Sky*, 1942. *From the Frank Driggs Collection.*

Eddie "Rochester" Anderson, Red Skelton, Duke Ellington, and Lena Horne backstage off the set of *Cabin in the Sky*, 1942. *From the Frank Driggs Collection.*

(Right) Lena Horne with Fats Waller in *Stormy Weather*, 1943. *From the Frank Driggs Collection.*

(Below) With Babe Wallace in *Stormy Weather*, 1943. *Photo courtesy of Duncan P. Schiedt.*

With dancer in *Broadway Rhythm*, 1943. *From the Frank Driggs Collection.*

Lena Horne and the cast off the set of *I Dood It.* Hazel Scott is at the piano. 1943. *From the Frank Driggs Collection.*

(Above) In *Two Girls and a Sailor*, 1944. *From the Frank Driggs Collection.*

(Left) With Joe Louis at the May-fair Room of the Blackstone Hotel in Chicago, June 4, 1949. *United Press International Photo.*

7

Lena Moves to Hollywood

*F*elix Young, manager of the not-yet-opened Club Trocadero, rented an apartment in Hollywood for Lena and her family. Being white and a non-racist, he had selected an apartment in a nice neighborhood that also happened to be all white. Cousin Edwina was so light complected that none of the neighbors on Horn Avenue looked twice at her, but they had some suspicions about Lena and Gail. They were not quite white—were they Spanish? Mulatto? Lena felt uncomfortable. Once the Club Trocadero opened and she started earning a salary, she would find a friendlier neighborhood.

The Club Trocadero did not open as scheduled. Felix Young was having trouble raising the necessary money. He kept the rent on Lena's apartment paid up and saw that she had money for food, but for all intents and purposes Lena and her family were living on charity. She didn't like that. She did not like being stranded in Los Angeles away from her friends and without a job.

Fortunately, Lena was not entirely without friends in Los Angeles. Duke Ellington was out there, doing a show called

Jump for Joy. He invited Lena to do a guest performance in his show and introduced her to Billy Strayhorn, a musician in his band who was also his chief music-writing collaborator. Even back in New York the Duke had told Lena that she and Billy ought to meet each other, and just as Ellington had expected, Lena and Billy hit it off right away. She found him easy to talk to, and she was amazed to find herself talking to him about herself. Ordinarily she did not talk much about herself, her thoughts and feelings, even with people she knew well. Billy was different; she trusted him instinctively right away. They talked about music and show business; they went to after-hours clubs like the Alabama to hear people like Winonie Harris sing the blues. When she was with Billy, Lena forgot her worries.

Lena and Billy were rehearsing together in a friend's home when news came over the radio that the United States had entered World War II. This unforeseen development destroyed all hopes for the opening of the Club Trocadero. Felix Young did, finally, open a smaller club called the "Little Troc" and tried to fit into it all the people to whom he'd promised jobs. But it was much too small for the Katherine Dunham dancers; they stumbled over tables and customers and simply could not dance in the tiny space. But the intimate atmosphere was perfect for Lena. Before long, big Hollywood stars like John Barrymore, Marlene Dietrich, Lana Turner and Steve Crane were frequenting the Little Troc and talking about its featured singer, Lena Horne.

The act Lena did at the Little Troc was essentially the same as the one she had been developing since her Cotton Club days. It was sensual and "sexy," and her repertoire consisted chiefly of popular white songs, although she occasionally threw in a light blues number. But the Hollywood reaction to her was entirely different from that in New York. In New York, her audiences had been able to separate a performer's onstage persona from the real person. Her Hollywood audiences thought that the Lena they saw onstage was the real Lena. She became the subject of Hollywood gossip, suspected of being a sexy siren offstage as well as on. The real Lena Horne went home to her daughter when she finished her shows. When she did go out socially, she was either with Billy Strayhorn or with another friend, singer Billie Daniels. But the Hollywood gossips had her going out with a different man every night. Lena was upset by the gossip, but she didn't know what she could do to stop it.

Fortunately, Teddy came for a visit, and so did the elder Teddy, Lena's father. Lena was so busy seeing to it that they enjoyed their time with her that she hardly thought about the gossip. The family did a lot of sightseeing together, and at night, after her shows at the Little Troc, Lena and her father went to various black night spots. People often commented that they made a "handsome couple," and Lena was proud to be seen with her father. She understood why her mother had fallen in love with him.

Soon afterward, Lena was offered a film contract by the movie company Metro-Goldwyn-Mayer. The company had acquired film rights to *Cabin in the Sky*, a Broadway play that had been directed by Vincente Minnelli, whom Lena had met while at Café Society Downtown. The plan was to produce an all-black film musical, and after a series of auditions that led to Lena's singing for Louis B. Mayer himself, Lena was offered a contract. By this time her father had returned to Pittsburgh, but Lena called him and asked him to come back. She wanted him to negotiate the contract for her. Perhaps he could help her avoid the problems she had experienced with her first Hollywood film. Also since M-G-M wanted her under contract not just for this one movie but for future movies as well, she wanted to make sure she didn't commit herself to playing roles that she considered undignified.

Returning straight away, Teddy Horne sat in on the contract negotiations and made it patently clear to the movie moguls that his daughter would not play roles that called for her to wait on some white star. He told them that he had enough money to hire someone to wait on his daughter if she wanted that. Lena felt confident that she would be able to avoid the stereotyped roles. She thought she was doing her job as a pioneer.

Unfortunately, the other black actors and actresses in Hollywood did not view her principled stand the way she did. In fact, they saw it as threatening to their own positions. They did not understand her attitude and thought that she was an "Eastern upstart" and "a tool of the NAACP." Lena was saddened and confused by the reaction of the other blacks; she did not understand why they did not applaud her for demanding certain dignity in her movie roles. But the only black in Hollywood who did not criticize her was Hattie McDaniel, a well-known actress who had made over twenty films in the 1930s and won an Academy Award as best supporting actress for her portrayal of the role of the mammy in *Gone with the Wind*. Hattie McDaniel had resented having always to play mammies and other servant roles and being denied the opportunity to show her talent in other roles. She befriended Lena and helped her through a difficult period, and since Duke Ellington and Billy Strayhorn had gone back East, Lena was especially grateful for this new friendship.

The ringleaders of the attack on Lena were the "captains", a small group of black performers who had organized themselves into an unofficial union and who took it upon themselves to act as go-betweens in relations between the studios and black actors and actresses. The studios would call these bosses and ask them to get a certain number of people to work for a stated number of days. In return, they were given the biggest parts and the most work. The captains were afraid that Lena's independent stand might disturb their system of favoritism. All of the other black performers depended on this handful of influential blacks, and if they got any ideas about standing up for themselves from Lena's example the old system might become ineffective. They ostracized Lena, and she knew that the captains would never suggest her for a role when the movie studios contacted them.

Being under contract with M-G-M was good for Lena at first. Although filming of *Cabin in the Sky* was delayed, she began collecting the two-hundred-dollar-a week salary called for in the contract as soon as that document was signed. Meanwhile, she did a musical number directed by Vincente Minnelli in a film called *Panama Hattie*.

The movie was essentially a white film, with white stars, Ann Sothern and Red Skelton. Although Lena appeared in the same film as they did, she never worked with them, never even saw them on the set. The segment of the movie in which she appeared was designed so that it was not integral to the story; the movie could be shown without it. It was designed this way because in those days, particularly in the South, white moviegoers did not want to see blacks in movies except as servants. If Lena's segment had been integrated into the movie script, many theaters would not have shown it. As designed, it could easily be cut out of the movie. Critics who did see *Panama Hattie* in its entirety were impressed by Lena. According to Gary Null, author of *Black Hollywood: The Negro in Motion Pictures*, Lena "made a tremendous impact with her remarkable voice" in that short segment. Critic Harrison Carroll wrote: "Best production number in the picture features the sultry Negro singer, Lena Horne."

Although she was pleased by this favorable critical reaction, Lena longed to have friends around her with whom she could share her success. But except for Hattie McDaniel, the only real friend around was Joe Louis, who was stationed at a nearby

Army camp. They saw a lot of each other, but Lena still felt lonely and discouraged by the snubs she received from most of the other black actors and actresses in Hollywood. She longed to be back in New York. Learning that there was to be a benefit at Café Society Downtown, she decided on impulse to return just for a few days.

Not until she actually arrived in New York did she realize how much she had missed the city and her friends. Both Billy Strayhorn and Billie Daniels escorted her to the benefit, and at the door she fell into the arms of Barney Josephson and burst into tears. Josephson had forgiven her for going to Hollywood, and theirs was a fine reunion. Bandleader Count Basie, another friend from Lena's time at Café Society Downtown, also attended the benefit; it was an evening of reunions. In fact, Lena did not want it to end. When it did end, she tearfully told Count Basie that she wasn't going back to Hollywood. But the Count told her she must. "They've never been given the chance to see a Negro woman as a woman," he said, referring to both moviemakers and movie audiences. "You've got to give them that chance." So, Lena returned to the West Coast.

Soon, however, she was back in New York. The management of the Savoy Plaza Hotel invited her to perform there, and since filming of *Cabin in the Sky* had been further delayed, M-G-M was persuaded to let her go. Her engagement at the Savoy Plaza reminded Lena of the aspect of New York that she did not miss: the segregation of its downtown hotels. Although she could perform at the Savoy, and had the use of a suite as her dressing room, she was barred as a guest. She stayed uptown at the Theresa.

During one performance at the Savoy, Lena became ill and collapsed, and the hotel manager offered to let her stay at the hotel that night. But Lena was not so sick that her pride was affected. If she couldn't stay there when she was well, she wasn't going to stay there when she was sick. She went uptown to the Theresa and summoned a doctor to treat her there. She returned to the Savoy Plaza the next night to find the embarrassed manager very apologetic and begging her to stay there for the rest of her engagement. Again she refused. Every night for the remainder of her engagement she gave her performance, then swept dramatically out of the hotel on her way to Harlem. But though she further embarrassed the hotel management in this way, she found little personal comfort in making such dramatic gestures. It was hard not to be bitter. By this time the United States was deeply embroiled in World War II, and black soldiers were overseas fighting for their country. Yet back home, in the most liberal and sophisticated city in the United States, a black person was denied the right to stay in a downtown hotel.

Some good things came out of Lena's engagement at the Savoy Plaza. She received excellent critical reviews. *Time* and *Life* carried articles about her, and for the first time she received nationwide publicity. Also during this time she met Zulme O'Neill, who was to become a lifelong friend.

At a party at the Theresa one afternoon, Lena noticed a woman whom she thought was white and immediately disapproved of such a woman hanging around black men. She decided the woman was a tramp and treated her accordingly. In response, the woman was nasty to Lena. Later, Lena learned that Zulme O'Neill was black and a graduate of Howard University, a black institution. Embarrassed to have had her own prejudices exposed, and to have made an incorrect assumption about the woman's character based on the color of her skin, Lena apologized. They became good friends. Zulme later married Cab Calloway, and Lena was godmother to the couple's first child.

Lena returned to Hollywood to begin filming at last on *Cabin in the Sky*, a movie whose production had been delayed so long primarily because it was considered a somewhat risky venture.

Great care had been taken to ensure its success even before filming began. It was risky because it was an all-black picture, and as a rule Hollywood was a stranger to all-black feature films. *The Duke Is Tops*, Lena's first Hollywood picture, had been a low-budget, "quickie" musical. A major, all-black dramatic film project would not even have been considered in Hollywood then. *Cabin* was a musical and so it accommodated the prevailing notion that blacks were always singing and dancing. Also, it had already enjoyed a respectable run as a musical on Broadway in 1940. But Arthur Freed, producer of the film version of *Cabin*, realized that even these advantages were not enough to sell the film to movie audiences. He needed people to work on the film who were right for it, and thus he gave Vincente Minnelli, who had directed the Broadway show, his first movie-directing job. He also cast Ethel Waters and Rex Ingram in the same roles that they had created for the Broadway *Cabin*.

In the Broadway version, Katherine Dunham had played the temptress, Georgia Brown, but Lena was hired for the part in the movie. Arthur Freed had heard Lena sing when she had first auditioned for the M-G-M bosses, and it was he who had arranged for her to sing for Louis B. Mayer himself on that same day. He had also urged M-G-M to sign her to a long-term contract. Freed believed that Lena Horne was right not just for the movie version of *Cabin* but for stardom, although the success of *Cabin* on the silver screen was uppermost in his mind.

Wrote Olive Graham in *Cinema Texas*, April 2, 1980: "There is no question that the caliber of the talent displayed in the cast was of the quality demanded by an M-G-M top feature. These actors were not novices, and all brought significant career experiences to their roles. Many of the minor characters in the film had stage and cabaret reputations equal to those in the leading roles, something not characteristic of musical casts. Louis Armstrong, 'Buck and Bubbles' (Ford Washington and

John Sublett), and the Duke Ellington Orchestra all were nationally known at this time."

Given all this talent, it was unfortunate that the plot of *Cabin in the Sky* was full of racial stereotypes. Blacks were portrayed as spending a lot of time singing and dancing and drinking too much and getting into fights. It featured Little Joe Jackson (played by Eddie Anderson) as a husband who is prone to straying from the straight and moral life his wife (Ethel Waters) tries to maintain. Lucifer, the devil (played by Rex Ingram), and the soldiers of heaven battle over Little Joe's soul. One of Lucifer's best weapons is Georgia Brown (played by Lena), a temptress who tries to seduce Little Joe away from his wife.

The studio's idea of a temptress was a woman with darker skin than Lena had. They were afraid that she would photograph "too white," and that would never do: white moviegoers, not to mention black ones, would object to a white-looking woman seducing a Negro man. So, the makeup people put dark makeup on Lena's skin. A special shade of pancake makeup was developed just for Lena. It was called "Light Egyptian," and Lena did not appreciate having to wear it. Nor, for that matter, did she appreciate playing a stereotyped Negro role (in the movies, if black women were not servants, then they were prostitutes). But she went along with the stereotype and the makeup she had to wear to conform to it. At least she was not playing a servant; and at least this role was integral to the film. She wasn't just appearing in some musical segment that could be cut out of the film if necessary.

She enjoyed working on the film. She had a solid reputation with the makeup people, wardrobe people, and other technicians on the set. Many of them had worked with her on *Panama Hattie*, and they regarded her as a "pro" because she was always on time, knew her lines, and was very cooperative. Lena also found it very exciting to be around and work with all the talented and experienced members of the cast—everyone, that is, except Ethel Waters.

Ethel Waters had a reputation for being hard to get along with, and Lena recalls that for her it was particularly hard. Although legend has it that Ethel and Lena met back in the Cotton Club days and that Ethel, hearing the teenaged Lena imitate her singing style, complimented her singing, Lena recalls that it was on the *Cabin* movie set that she tried imitating Waters's style and that the older star was not pleased. In fact, Ethel Waters was insulted. She resented other black female singers, and particularly resented Lena for having had it easier than she: for not having worked as long and as hard as she had to get into a Hollywood movie. The two women were scheduled to appear in only a couple of scenes together, and they avoided one another at other times. Lena recalls that she took particular care not to offend Ethel Waters again. But one day she had an accident on the set; her foot was placed in a cast. Waters resented the extra attention Lena received because of the accident, and when someone offered Lena a pillow on which to prop her injured foot, Waters blew up. Her fierce outburst shook up everyone, and the entire production was shut down for a day. Filming resumed the next day, but the two women did not speak to one another after that.

Cabin in the Sky premiered at the Capitol Theater in New York in 1943. The lines of people waiting to get in to see the all-black musical were so long that the usually cool Duke Ellington, a man who had met with royalty, was visibly moved by the attention. Lena was beside herself with excitement about her "homecoming." This time there was no Louis around to forbid her to participate in the festivities, and she basked in the warmth of success. Critics were kind to her, calling her portrayal of Georgia Brown "alluring" and "seductive." They were not so generous in their appraisal of the movie, however. Black critics condemned it for perpetuating racial stereotypes. Nowadays, despite its drawbacks, it is considered a classic in film history. Wrote Gary Null, "As the first all-black musical in many years, it was a major achievement in both form and content. Director Vincente Minnelli expanded the stage musical into what many critics have felt was the best black musical ever made. It fused a strong book with delightful music, including songs like 'Taking a Chance on Love,' 'Happiness is Just a Thing Called Joe,' and 'Life's Full of Consequences.' "

During the months between the time that filming of *Cabin in the Sky* was finished and the time that the movie actually premiered, Lena kept busy. Able to afford to live in a better neighborhood now that she had a guaranteed salary from M-G-M, she moved away from her unfriendly neighbors to an area of Horn Avenue east of Sunset Boulevard where other Hollywood stars lived. Many of her new neighbors, though wealthier and better educated than the migrants from Oklahoma and Arkansas who had been her neighbors, were equally unfriendly. In fact, some of them circulated a petition to force her and her family out. But others came to her support, among them Peter Lorre. Humphrey Bogart threatened to hit the person who sought his signature on the petition. The attempt to force Lena and her family out failed, and they settled down to living as best they could in the unfriendly town of Hollywood. But Lena smarted at the idea that anyone would actually take up a petition against her, and she soon became involved with organizations that worked for black rights in Hollywood. Perhaps following in her grandmother's footsteps, she joined HICCASP (Hollywood Independent Citizens Committee of the Arts, Sciences, and Professions) and worked with California Assemblyman Gus Hawkins for the establishment of a Fair Employment Practices Commission in California.

Because she was under contract with M-G-M, Lena had an easier time getting work than other black actors and actresses in Hollywood, and fortunately she did not have to rely on the good will of the captains, which she had lost practically as soon as she had arrived. Between the time filming was completed on *Cabin* and the premiere of the movie, she worked on two more films.

M-G-M "loaned" her to 20th Century-Fox to do *Stormy Weather*, another all-black film in which Fox wanted to showcase the talents of Bill "Bojangles" Robinson, the extraordinary dancer who was the most famous black entertainer of the time. Lena played his girlfriend in a thin story that revolved around their romance and that provided for lots of singing and dancing, as was expected in black films. Cab Calloway and his band appeared in the film, as did Katherine Dunham and her dance troupe. Jazz pianist Fats Waller and the Nicholas Brothers, a dancing team, were also featured.

Lena sang the title song of the movie. "Stormy Weather," the song, was a sad song, actually a blues song about the breakup of a romance. To be effective, it had to be sung with genuine feeling, and Lena could not seem to summon the necessary emotion. Although she had come to understand and appreciate the history of blues music, under the tutelage of Barney Josephson in New York, she still did not know how to sing the blues. Realizing that she needed help, Cab Calloway took her aside just before she was supposed to do the number for the camera. He told her to think about her own marital problems. Then, for good measure, he called her a few dirty names. Properly upset, Lena sang "Stormy Weather" with the feeling the song required. Hers was a moving rendition, and the song became her trademark. Even today, whenever she appears, she is asked to sing "Stormy Weather."

Before filming on *Stormy Weather* began, Lena recorded with Hazel Scott the music for a big, complicated musical number that was to be part of *I Dood It*, an M-G-M black musical starring Dooley Wilson. Neither Hazel nor Lena liked the way the conductor was handling the musical arrangements, feeling that he was taking much too long to get the music recorded. Kay Thompson, an M-G-M vocal coach, mentioned that she wished Lennie Hayton had done the arrangements. If he had, she said, things would have been a lot easier for all of them.

Lena wondered briefly about that remark. She had seen Lennie Hayton, who worked as an arranger for M-G-M, around. They had exchanged polite nods. But Lena had gotten the impression that Lennie didn't like her, and since she had not done anything to make him dislike her, she did not think she liked him. She certainly didn't dwell on the matter; she had more important things to worry about than whether or not some white musical arranger liked her.

After she finished her work on *Stormy Weather*, Lena returned to M-G-M to shoot the actual film sequence with Hazel Scott for *I Dood It*. This film, too, was directed by Vincente Minnelli, and Lena enjoyed working with him again. One day she, Vincente, and a group of other "transplanted New Yorkers" were having lunch in the M-G-M commissary when Lennie Hayton walked in and joined the group. Lena later recalled, "I guess it would be fair to say that we really saw each other for the first time. . . . It was like the recognition scene in the movies, when the boy and girl, in a blinding flash, realize that they like each other after all." Later that same afternoon, Lennie came by the set to watch Lena work. He didn't stay long, just stood there a few minutes, watching, then left. The scene they were working on was finished the next day, and Lena, Hazel, Vincente, and some of the other people who had worked on the musical number went out to celebrate at the Francis Edwards Restaurant across the street. Lennie showed up again, and this time Vincente invited him to join the party.

Soon after that, Lennie went over to the piano and started to play, and Lena and Hazel began to sing. Lena was impressed by Lennie's vast repertoire; it seemed to her that he knew all of the songs she'd ever heard. She was even more impressed when she learned that he had arranged the music for her favorite recording of "Stardust" by Artie Shaw, which she had often asked to be played on the radio back in New York. After a while, the others left, but Lena and Lennie remained. Within a few weeks they were seeing each other constantly.

8
Battling Hollywood Prejudice

*L*ena *felt* more comfortable with Lennie Hayton than she had ever felt with any other man, black or white. He was a quiet man and a loner and was so absorbed in his music that he rarely associated with people who were not part of the music world. And he judged these people not on the basis of their personality, or of their color, but of their music. Lena admired this quality in Lennie. She valued his opinions and considered him her best friend. Although she had been brought up not to trust white people, she found it easy to trust Lennie. When she was with him, she did not think about their racial differences.

Unfortunately, she could not persuade Cousin Edwina to feel the same way. When Cousin Edwina saw the fondness developing between Lena and Lennie she issued an ultimatum: Lena must choose between Lennie and her. It was a hard choice for Lena to make. Her father's cousin had been with her ever since she had left Charlie Barnet's band and Lena had grown to depend on her. Edwina had taken good care of Gail and Teddy, who was now living on a semi-permanent basis with Lena because Louis had moved to California but was not yet settled. But Lena was also determined not to bow to racial prejudice any more than was necessary, and in her opinion her cousin's racial prejudice was not worth forsaking her belief that she had a right to spend time with a friend, no matter what his color. She told Edwina that she would not stop seeing Lennie, and Edwina packed up and left.

Luckily, just about the time Edwina left, Lena met Mrs. Ida Starks, whose husband was in the Army and who was alone with her daughter. The two women realized immediately that they could develop a mutually rewarding relationship. Mrs. Starks was very lonely, and Lena needed someone to take care of her children. Mrs. Starks and her daughter moved into Lena's house.

Just after Mrs. Starks moved in, Lena's children had an experience that Lena had tried to forestall as long as possible. One day, Gail and Teddy and Mrs. Starks's little girl came home from school in tears. Their kindergarten and first grade class-mates had called them "Nigger." Lena quieted the children and told them that they did not have to go back to school for a few days. Then she went off by herself to think about the situation that she had known would have to be faced from the moment she had enrolled the children in the otherwise all-white school. The next day, Lena went to the school to talk with Gail's teacher, who was sympathetic about what had happened. She blamed the trouble on the "Okies" and "Arkies." Lena suggested that the teacher might use what had happened to teach the children the right way to treat each other, to behave kindly to one another regardless of race. But the teacher said she didn't think she could teach that lesson. Lena decided not to send the children back to that school.

Ever since she had moved her family to Hollywood, Lena had worried about how the racism there would affect her children.

She had moved east on Horn Avenue because she had not wanted to expose them to racial insults. But they were exposed to them anyway in the school in their new, supposedly "better" neighborhood. She decided there was no use trying to raise her children in Hollywood. She would move back to New York, where they would have a better chance of escaping some of the worst aspects of racism. The move would not greatly affect her movie career, for the little work she got took only a few weeks out of the year. She could commute to Hollywood for that. Her old friend, Cab Calloway, helped her find a house in St. Albans, in the borough of Queens. The neighborhood was in transition— white middle-class people were moving out and black middle-class people were moving in—and Lena hoped it would be a friendly environment for her family.

Mrs. Starks decided that she and her daughter would go to New York, too, and Lena was in the process of arranging for the move when her mother and Mike showed up in Hollywood. Back in Cuba, they had gotten the impression that Lena was a big Hollywood star, and they did not think that the money she had been sending them was enough. So, they had decided to go to Hollywood and make sure Edna received a proper reward for her sacrifices on behalf of her daughter's early career. They checked into a Hollywood hotel that did not admit blacks and called Lena to pick them up. Lena called Lennie. If she walked into the lobby of that hotel, the management might suspect that her mother was not white. Lennie went into the hotel to get Lena's mother and Mike, while Lena waited outside in the car.

As soon as she got into the car, Lena's mother began to demand that Lena get in touch with some movie producers on her behalf; she had not given up her dream to be an actress and believed that her famous daughter could now help her. She did not believe Lena when she explained that she did not have a close relationship with a single producer. Lena tried to get her mother to understand that in Hollywood terms she was a very minor figure. Her refusal to play servant roles limited the number of parts she was offered. Even though she was under contract to M-G-M, she did not get regular movie work, for M-G-M was just like the other major studios: it did white movies with occasional servant roles for blacks, or it did "race" movies, and it did very few "race" movies. In fact, M-G-M had so little work for her that the studio had arranged for her to go on a singing tour of the Loew's Theater Circuit. Her appearance in M-G-M movies had brought her to national attention and caused white audiences to accept her as a performer, although they still rejected her race. When Edna and Mike showed up, Lena was getting ready to leave on the tour.

But her mother remained unconvinced that she had no influence in Hollywood. While Lena was out of town touring, Edna went to her daughter's home and demanded that Mrs. Starks hand over Lena's personal telephone book; she wanted to find the names and numbers of movie producers. Mrs. Starks refused, and the two women had a terrible fight. When Lena learned what had happened, she went to her lawyers and asked them to work out an arrangement to send her mother more money. Apparently Edna was placated, because she and her husband returned to Cuba. Lena, Mrs. Starks, and the children moved to St. Albans, Queens.

By the time Lena and her entourage arrived in New York, it was 1945 and the United States was fighting on both the Pacific and European fronts. The nation had united behind the war effort, and the people of Hollywood did their part by going on USO (United Service Organization) tours to entertain American troops on U.S. bases. In this Hollywood effort, Lena was happy to be involved. She had always been willing to perform at benefits for many and varied causes, and the cause of American servicemen seemed to her especially worthwhile. She was glad that whatever stardom she had achieved had come at a time when she could represent her people in a meaningful way. She was proud to have the honor of christening the *George Washington Carver*, a Liberty Ship that would have a black captain and that was named for a famous black agricultural scientist who is best known for finding many uses for peanuts and peanut oil. She was happy to be a "pinup girl" for black soldiers who would have gotten into serious trouble if they had displayed posters and pictures of white Hollywood stars like Hedy Lamarr or Betty Grable, as the white soldiers did. She was flattered when the airmen of the all-black Ninety-Ninth Squadron crowned her "queen of the Ninety-Ninth."

Performers on USO-sponsored tours entertained both white and black soldiers, and Lena did not mind that. But she did mind the segregated practices in the Army, and the way black soldiers were discriminated against when they were putting their lives on the line for their country. She resented having to perform for the white troops first; it bothered her that the performances for the black troops were given in separate, and less adequate, facilities.

Once, while touring with Horace Henderson, brother of the band leader Fletcher Henderson, Lena went to Fort Riley, Kansas. In the afternoon, they performed for the white soldiers in a huge auditorium. She expected to perform for the black soldiers later in the day and then to leave for home, and she was angry to learn that the performance for them had been scheduled for the following day and that she would have to remain overnight at Fort Riley. The next day, she grew angrier still when she saw the tiny, segregated mess hall and the makeshift stage where she was to perform for the black troops. Then she grew puzzled. The front rows of seats were occupied by white men. Turning to the black soldier who had been assigned to escort her and the band, she demanded to know who those white men were. "They're German prisoners of war," he said.

Lena was infuriated and insulted; her dignity as an American was offended. The idea of having the enemy sit in the front rows because they were white! She marched down from the platform and positioned herself so that she was facing the black troops, with her back to the POWs. She began to sing directly to the black soldiers, but she could not regain her self-control. Tired from the long tour, and deeply hurt by the humiliation to which both she and the black soldiers had been subjected, she was so choked with emotion that she was unable to continue. She walked away in tears.

Lena announced that she would not accept any further assistance from the Army and would no longer travel on Army planes. She wired home for money to pay her own travel expenses. Lena also wired the Hollywood branch of the USO to tell her sponsors that she was quitting the tour. With that done, Lena visited the local NAACP office, where she explained what had happened at Fort Riley. There she met Daisy Bates, who later gained national attention in the campaign to integrate the public schools in Little Rock, Arkansas. Daisy Bates told Lena that the NAACP was aware of the problems at the base and was working to make conditions better for black soldiers; but such things took time, and had to be done carefully. Lena was not placated, but there was little that she could do.

Back in Hollywood, Lena was reprimanded by two of the sponsoring organizations for the USO tours. The word went out that she was to be kept out of southern camps, but that order did not stop Lena. She paid her own expenses to travel to southern camps and entertain the black soldiers at them. In California, she became involved in the campaign for housing for wounded Japanese-Americans who, like others of their heritage, faced great discrimination in the United States after Japanese planes attacked the U.S. fleet at Pearl Harbor in Hawaii in December 1941. In California, where there was a large population of Japanese-Americans, many of these United States citizens were forced into internment camps during the war. Even those who returned wounded from fighting in the war on the American side were denied adequate housing. Lena supported them in their bid for fair treatment.

At the same time as she was trying to help other victims of discrimination, Lena herself continued to feel personally the effects of racism. By agreement with M-G-M, she performed frequently at clubs and hotels in various parts of the country, and many times she suffered a humiliation similar to that which she had experienced in Boston when she was with Noble Sissle and in New York at the Savoy Plaza. Some hotels where she performed would not accept her as a guest. Some let her stay during her engagement but barred her from using the main lobby elevator. Some allowed her to stay but refused to give rooms to the black musicians who accompanied her. It seemed that everywhere she turned she ran into an affront, either to her own dignity or to that of other human beings. And as if all this were not enough, she was embroiled in divorce proceedings and a custody fight with Louis over Teddy.

Lennie Hayton became even more important to her during this period. He listened to her and seemed to understand her pain, but did not try to offer a lot of advice. He respected the fact that she was an independent person who needed to make her own decisions and did not try to control her in any way. Even maintaining a relationship with Lennie was difficult for Lena. Interracial dating was taboo in American society, and the two rarely appeared together in public. Lena did not want Lennie to come to her home very often, because of the children. But they managed to see each other, and to talk, and Lena credits Lennie with helping her to preserve her sanity when it seemed that everything around her was going haywire.

She needed him especially when her fight with Louis over custody of Teddy came to a climax. It had been a long-running battle, and Lena lost. For years afterward she wondered what she might have done differently. Before there had been any serious talk of divorce, Louis had moved to California and suggested to Lena that he be her agent. Lena didn't like that idea, for black agents were almost nonexistent in Hollywood and the few around had no real influence. Although she tried to explain how the system worked to her husband, he was hurt and refused to understand. Divorce seemed inevitable, but once proceedings began Louis insisted on having custody of Teddy. In fact, he would not consent to a divorce unless he had primary custody of his son. Lena wanted to fight him in court, but her agents and attorneys warned her against doing so. A nasty custody battle would attract too much unfavorable publicity and hurt her family. It would also hurt her career. She would be portrayed as an ambitious woman who had deserted her husband when her career plans began to materialize. Public sympathy would be with Louis; public opinion would be against her, and not only she but her children would suffer for it. Thus, Lena agreed to a custody arrangement under which she would have Teddy only a few months out of the year. "And so," she wrote in her autobiography, "my son grew up as a partial stranger to me. . . . I am certain our love would have been stronger if we had been together more."

Once she had lost custody of Teddy, Lena wondered if she had received good advice from her attorneys, but there was not much she could do about it. In the months that followed, she also had reason to question if she had the right agents and managers. It seemed to her that they put her money-making ability above her concerns as a human being. A particularly upsetting incident occurred when M-G-M booked her into the Orpheum in Los Angeles, the first time she had ever played such a big theater in that city. Jimmie Lunceford and his band were headlining the show, and Lena, who knew Lunceford from the Cotton Club, was excited about working with him again. She could not have asked for a better band to back her for her first big theater date in Los Angeles.

Arriving at the midnight rehearsal for the Orpheum show, she was prepared to give her best performance ever. Then one of the musicians told her that a talented black singer named June Richmond had been dropped from the show because of her. June Richmond was still a relatively unknown singer, while Lena Horne had appeared in movies and had far more "star quality." Lena was mortified to learn that her big chance had come at the expense of someone else's. But it was too late to back out, and there was no point in trying to convince June Richmond that she had not connived to steal the booking away from her. On opening night, June Richmond was right there in the front row, staring up at her accusingly.

Lena blamed her management for placing her in such an embarrassing position. No one had bothered to tell her that she was bumping June Richmond from a spot on the Orpheum bill. She blamed her management, too, for failing to include in her performance contracts details that would protect her from racial slights. She felt that they ought to include such things as how she and her band would be treated so she would not arrive at some hotel and be told she couldn't use the main elevator. She also resented her managers's failure to take into account her concern for her own people.

Shortly after she closed at the Orpheum Theater in Los Angeles, Lena was booked into the Howard Theater in Washington, D.C. It was a black theater and a famous one, and Lena's arrival in the city was attended by considerable fanfare. In fact, her reception by black press and white press was unique. The November 16, 1944, issue of the black *Los Angeles Sentinel* headlined the event:

LENA BRINGS COLORED, WHITE NEWSPAPERMEN
TOGETHER IN DEE CEE

Washington, D.C.—(NNPA)—Lena Horne came to Washington several days ahead of her engagement at the Howard Theater here and was the guest of honor at a press party thrown by the Lichtman Theaters management. The party was a riproaring success, and Lena was sensational in her beauty, her wit, her diplomatic side-stepping of questions aimed at uncovering her heart interests. But there was a more significant development.

Lena was unveiled, quite unintentionally, as a worthy ambassador of good will and better race relations for the Negro. Besides beauty, she has brains—and she uses them.

This correspondent was amazed at the fluent manner in which she intelligently discussed unions, politics, race relations, social welfare. And she was not parrot-like in repeating any set speeches.

She was expressing her own deep-seated sentiments and ideas.

She has an appreciation for the close similarity between the problems of organized labor and those of the Negro. She belongs to three unions—the radio guild, the actor's guild, and the screen guild. She told one reporter that if he chose to interpret it that way, she was perfectly willing for him to say she regarded her union membership as a type of insurance.

But here's an actual development for which Lena may be given credit. At the press party were representatives of the local white press—theater critics and even editors. No other person, very likely, could have drawn them there despite the cordial invitation extended.

Most of them had never come in personal contact with members of the Negro press before—or with any intelligent Negroes, for that matter. A few of them were so impressed that plans are now under way now for an interracial press luncheon so more of the 'white' press may learn what goes on.

> Yep, Lena's in there, pitching, and she's throwing strikes
> as well as curves.

Ordinarily, the Howard Theater shows were well attended, and given the pre-engagement publicity Lena had received she expected a standing-room-only crowd. But on opening night, the house was nearly empty. Lena was embarrassed, and worried. Until then, she had refused to believe the warnings from whites, and some blacks, in Hollywood that most black people would not accept her, that she was "too different, too Hollywood," for their tastes. But singing to a smattering of an audience can cause any performer to question his or her popularity and acceptability, and Lena had more reason than most performers to feel insecure.

Lena decided to find out for sure. She inquired about ticket prices and learned that her agents had arranged for tickets to her shows to be sold for the same steep prices that high-class white theaters charged. Ticket prices for her show at the Howard were higher than those charged when the famous jazz singer Ella Fitzgerald appeared. Lena was furious.

First, she called her managers in California and told them she would cancel her engagement if they did not agree to lower ticket prices. Then she met with the manager of the Howard Theater to work out a strategy to fill the house for her remaining shows. Together, they met with the press and Lena explained what had happened. There would be lower ticket prices for the rest of her engagement, she promised. The representatives of the press spread the word, and Lena's engagement at the Howard Theater turned out to be one of her most successful to date. Still, Lena could not forget that without her own personal efforts, it could have been a disaster. Her experience at the Howard Theater made her even more aware of her need for sensitive management that would take into account the special problems of her career. But she did not know where to find that kind of management, if indeed it even existed. And even if she did find it, she was still under contract to M-G-M, and M-G-M had primary control over her career.

In 1945, Arthur Freed, producer of all the M-G-M musicals in which Lena had appeared, contacted her about playing the lead role in a Broadway show to be called *St. Louis Woman*. The play was based on a book by two well-known black writers, Arna Bontemps and Countee Cullen, and the musical score was being written by the equally famous white team of Harold Arlen and Johnny Mercer. Freed showed Lena the music first. The score included the song "Come Rain or Come Shine," which remains popular today, and Lena loved the music. But when she read the script she had a different reaction; although it was based on the writings of blacks, the story had been altered to emphasize the usual Negro character clichés. The leading character was a stereotypical flashy whore, and Lena did not want to play that role. She told Freed that she wanted to play a role from real black life.

Freed and the people in power at M-G-M did not understand her misgivings. They felt that the role was a good vehicle for her talents. Besides, this was an opportunity for her to work, and since the company was paying her under the terms of her contract, the company expected her to perform for her pay. Some people who were sensitive to her need for dignity pointed out that Lena would open the way for more blacks to appear on Broadway, appealing to her sense of racial identity to get what they wanted.

But other voices urged Lena to hold firm in her refusal to play the St. Louis woman. Individuals, as well as organizations like the NAACP, reminded her that she must preserve her dignified image and not be a party to furthering racial stereotypes. Lena listened to all the voices, and found herself in a quandary. On the one hand, she wanted to work, wanted the opportunity to appear again on Broadway, loved the show's musical score, and wanted to please the bosses at M-G-M. On the other hand, she did not want to have any part in furthering the stereotypes that kept whites, and even some blacks, from seeing Negroes as human beings. In the end, she refused the role in *St. Louis Woman*.

The M-G-M people were furious at Lena. In retaliation, they refused to let her accept the offer of a good part in a Broadway revival of the musical *Show Boat*. Lena was heartbroken, for the part of Julie in *Show Boat* was just the type of role she wanted; it could be played by a black woman or a white woman and so was not a stereotyped role. M-G-M also denied her permission to work in cabarets. The only outside work they would agree to were appearances on the Loew's Theater circuit, because that was good for M-G-M's business. Each time Lena's requests to do outside work were denied, she became more angry and frustrated. It seemed to her that she was being punished for more than just her refusal to accept the role in *St. Louis Woman*. She suspected that her increasingly close relationship with Lennie Hayton also had something to do with the studio's negative attitude. But every time she tried to talk to one of the studio bosses about the situation, she was rebuffed.

The enforced idleness drove her crazy. So did her sense of being utterly powerless to do anything about it. To make matters worse, she was worried about her mounting expenses. She had recently purchased, with Lennie, a small house in the Nichols Canyon area of Los Angeles, primarily because it was a secluded place where they could be together, and the expense of maintaining homes on both coasts was high. In addition, she had to keep paying the three musicians who traveled with her on the Loew's Theater circuit, even when they had no bookings, because otherwise she would lose them.

One night Lena met Joan Crawford at a party. Ms. Crawford had heard of Lena's problems and she told Lena of having a similar problem at one time. She suggested that Lena find a bigger agency that had more "pull" with the studio. She also said that Lena should make a personal appeal to L. B. Mayer. Lena had already tried to do this and had been ignored; she didn't like the idea of trying it again. Joan Crawford pointed out to Lena that she herself, and other big name stars, too, had at one time or another gone "begging" to Louis Mayer. After all, it was his company and he ran it the way he wanted to. If Lena wanted to work again, she had to swallow her pride and ask him to let her do so; there was no getting around it.

Following this advice, Lena got Music Corporation of America to represent her, buying out her contract from her old agency with money advanced to her by MCA. MCA then worked to soften up the people around Louis Mayer so Lena could get in to see him. When she did, he cried over what he called her ungrateful attitude, but the long months of punishment came to an end after that meeting. Lena was allowed to work in cabarets again and to take other outside bookings.

9
Lena and Lennie Marry

During all of the problems with M-G-M, the divorce proceedings, and the worry over money, Lennie Hayton stood by Lena. He comforted her, and advised her when she asked his advice. Meanwhile, he also helped her professionally. He wrote arrangements for her that she felt were perfect for her voice and style. Under his tutelage, her voice gained strength, and she seemed to enjoy singing more every day. But her deepening attachment to him disturbed her. It was very difficult for a black woman and a white man to be close in the 1940s. Their relationship had already caused Cousin Edwina to leave, and she still did not feel that she could entertain Lennie in front of her children. She knew M-G-M disapproved of the relationship and she knew, too, that the few times they had appeared together in public had caused considerable gossip in Hollywood. Yet, she could not bring herself to give up a relationship that was becoming increasingly important to her.

As Lena became more deeply attached to Lennie, the question of color tormented her, and she experienced wide mood swings. On the one hand, she found herself telling objecting blacks of her rights as an individual and private person. On the other hand, her resentment over white racism would cause her to strike out at Lennie. She explained years later, "I would turn on Lennie, and he would be nothing but a convenient white whipping boy. 'You bastards think we're inferior? OK, I'll show you.' And then I would make his life hell for him. I gave him all the psychological punishment I could not give the rest of the white men. I took advantage of him. I demanded more of him than I would normally ask in any relationship."

When these ugly moods struck her, Lena would remember Edwina's warnings—the collective belief of black women—that white men never marry black women, they just use them. She would become blind to everything about him but his skin color and try to make him pay the accumulated debt of all whites. In response, he would calmly assure her that he loved her and wanted to marry her whenever she was ready. Often, this response just made her angrier, because it made her feel guilty. With Lennie, she sometimes felt caught in an emotional whirlpool.

In the meantime, Lena's problems as a black performer continued, among them problems with her new agency, MCA. MCA had helped Lena to persuade Louis Mayer and his company to let her work again. The agency also controlled bookings in some very important nightclubs, and in gaining entree for Lena in these clubs MCA helped open the door for other blacks to follow. But it soon became apparent to Lena that her new agency treated her differently from its white clients.

The good luck telegram never arrived on opening night as was the tradition when the performer was white. The local MCA representative never showed up before the third or fourth night to check out working conditions. Lena and her musicians would often arrive to work in a hotel where she could stay, but her black musicians could not, or where none of them could use the front entrance. MCA showed no more willingness to forestall these indignities by writing into her contracts specific arrangements about working conditions than her old agency had. The people at MCA were not sensitive to the special problems she faced.

In 1945, MCA booked her into the Copacabana in New York City. It was an important engagement, for Lena Horne was the first black entertainer invited to perform in the club's main room. Lena was excited about this breakthrough engagement, and thrilled to be performing in New York for the first time since 1942. On opening night, the audience was large, and appreciative, but amidst her joy over her success Lena nevertheless noticed that the audience contained no blacks. The picket lines outside the club told her why: blacks who tried to gain admittance to the Copacabana were turned away with the excuse, "Sorry, but we have no record of your reservations."

Lena hated having been made an unwitting party to segregation. She tried to break her contract, and when she found that she could not legally do so she wrote a public statement explaining her position. She could not break her present contract, she explained, but she made it clear that any future contracts she signed with the Copacabana would contain a guarantee that no one would be barred from seeing her act because of race. She returned to the Copacabana in 1946. Lennie took a leave of absence from M-G-M to serve as her conductor. This time, as Lena had promised, blacks were admitted.

By 1947, Lena and Lennie had decided to get married. They both realized that they faced many difficulties as an interracial couple, but they needed each other enough to risk those difficulties. Once they had decided to marry, they also decided that it would be unwise to do so in the United States; they were sure there would be ugly reactions. Instead, they went to

Europe, and in October 1947, accompanied by Tiny Kyle, Lena's hairdresser, and Luther Henderson, her pianist, they set sail for England. Lena had arranged some bookings in London and Paris; while in Europe she and Lennie would get married.

In London, Lena was booked at a small Soho club called the London Casino. She hired local musicians to accompany her and found that her act was very popular among the artists and intellectuals who patronized the club. Soon, she and Lennie were being invited to parties and other events and meeting English writers, actors, and painters, among them the famous poet-philosopher Dylan Thomas. Lena found these people to be warm and friendly and far more interested in talent than in skin color.

Unfortunately, other segments of London's population were not so welcoming. The Piccadilly Hotel gave Lena a room because she was a star, but refused to accommodate Tiny and Luther. Lena had to put up a fight to get the management of the hotel to relent and accommodate her entire party. Then the management turned around and refused to admit some West Indians. There was growing resentment among white Londoners toward the influx of dark-skinned people from British territories in the West Indies. They were British subjects, but in England they were not treated as first-class citizens. Lena criticized the attitude of the whites in Britain when she was interviewed by British reporters.

Lena and everyone else in her party were relieved when they left London for Paris. By making the brief crossing of the English Channel they entered an entirely different world where racial attitudes were concerned. Lena's Paris agent met them in front of the Raphaël Hotel and personally saw that they were all checked in. The whole process went so smoothly that Lena would have had pleasant memories of the hotel even if it had been a "flea bag."

But the Raphaël was Paris's best, and Lena will never forget the experience of staying there. The suite into which she was ushered through heavy wooden doors reminded her of a fairy-tale palace. A magnificent crystal chandelier hung in the sitting room. The walls and even the lampshades were covered in silk. The bedroom had chaise lounges for resting; the bedspread and drapes were red silk taffeta. In the sitting room, an elegant cold buffet was spread out on the table, and when Lena pulled the silk cord that hung next to the bed, a maid appeared to serve her. Lena had never stayed in such a luxurious place before. Years earlier, when she had taken ill at the Savoy Plaza in New York, the room offered to her for her recovery had been spartan compared to this.

On the streets of Paris, Lena enjoyed another kind of luxury—the ability to walk along the street with Lennie and not be the object of stares. The French people showed no special interest in them; they were free to just "be" for the first time, and they loved it. Americans who had been to Paris before World War II found the post-war city a sad and less welcoming place than the one they remembered, but to Lena and Lennie Paris in late 1947 was the earthbound equivalent of heaven.

After a few days of sightseeing, Lena went to work at the Club Champs-Elysée for two weeks. After that, they all went to Liége, in Belgium, where Lena was engaged for a few days at the elegant Chaudfontaine Spa. On their return to Paris, Lena and Lennie got married. He and Luther Henderson had made most of the arrangements before they had left for Belgium. All that remained was for Lennie to buy the wedding ring, but neither he nor Luther expected that to be a problem. In fact, while Lena was dressing for the wedding, Lennie ran out to get the ring. He was astonished to find that there was a gold shortage in post-war Paris, and jewelers did not have gold wedding bands. Frantic, he tried jeweler after jeweler, with no luck. Meanwhile, Lena waited in the hotel room, fretting that Lennie had decided not to go through with the wedding after all. At last Lennie found a jeweler with a sense of romance and who was sympathetic to his pleas. He got the ring and rushed back for the ceremony. Lena wore black, just as she had for her first wedding, and cried throughout the brief ceremony.

Almost immediately, they set sail for New York, arriving in New York Harbor December 22, 1947. As soon as they had boarded the ship they had agreed to put the freedom they had enjoyed in Paris out of their minds and to concentrate on the realities that awaited them in the United States. Still, they found it difficult to return home, for although they had decided to keep their marriage a secret from the public, they had agreed that it was only fair to tell their families, and Lena, for one, was not looking forward to the reaction of her relatives.

When they heard the news, most of her family stopped speaking to her. She was particularly hurt by her father's refusal to accept her marriage to a white man. Lennie's mother was kind and loving toward Lena, and Lena was grateful for that. The rest of the world, black and white, was not told about the marriage. There were rumors, of course, but neither Lena nor Lennie, nor their families nor the few close friends who knew, would confirm them. Fear of the nasty public reaction to her marriage caused Lena to choose to appear to live in sin with a white man rather than to say publicly that he was her husband.

She worried more about the reaction of black people than she did about that of white people. She was accustomed to white rejection. What she feared she would not be able to take was the reaction of her own family multiplied a thousandfold and echoing across the country. She realized that she was already distrusted by black Americans; they had never seen a black as successful in Hollywood and with white audiences as she had been, and they were naturally suspicious of her. They saw her as a Hollywood glamour girl and suspected that she was a "white

Negro" who had sold out her race. All the public protests against discrimination and segregation she had made had not erased this suspicion. She feared that her marriage, even though it was an entirely personal matter, might sever her ties with black people permanently. Having severed her ties with most of her own family by marrying Lennie, she was unwilling to lose the larger, impersonal family of her race.

It was fairly easy to keep the secret of their marriage. Lennie was still under contract with M-G-M and based in California. Lena's "home" was in St. Albans, Queens, with Gail. When she was not there, she was usually on the road. Occasionally, she and Lennie were able to spend a long weekend together at the house in Nichols Canyon, but even these times together were soon marred by the racism of their neighbors.

The neighbors had been wondering about the new owners of the house ever since it had been sold. Once they got a good look at Lena, they were furious. They took up a petition to have her ejected from the neighborhood. Some even threatened violence. Lena bought a shotgun. She and Lennie built a high wall around the property. The neighborhood protests died down after a while. People clucked disapprovingly about what they imagined Lena and Lennie were doing behind the high walls, but they left them alone. In their enforced privacy, Lena and Lennie enjoyed as much time together as they could, and sometimes entertained trusted friends. But it was not enough for either of them, and the years of separation and of being secretly married were very difficult for them both.

Lena especially missed her husband when she was on the road and suffering the indignities that had plagued her career from the start. She still came face to face with discrimination and segregation almost everywhere she went, and she was continually frustrated in her efforts to persuade her agents to be more racially sensitive. She tried not to burden Lennie with her problems, but he sensed that she was having a hard time, and he decided that she ought to have a personal manager on the road with her. He persuaded their friend, Ralph Harris, to stop plugging songs for the big record companies and to take over as Lena's manager.

Once again, Lena arranged to buy her contract from an agency that did not work for her best interests. Free of MCA, she allowed Ralph Harris to take over the management of her career, and almost immediately she felt many burdens lift from her shoulders. Ralph Harris did not need to be told that special clauses had to be written into Lena's performance contracts to protect her from discrimination. He saw to it that black organizations in the cities where she appeared were notified in advance. He sent press releases to the black newspapers. Lena's former agents had not bothered to do these things, and their lack of action had reflected on Lena personally. Once Ralph Harris took over management, Lena saw a change in attitude toward her on the part of the black press and black organizations. They were less suspicious of her, less inclined to judge her a "white Negro" who had sold out her own people for success.

Ralph Harris understood Lena's need to "connect" with her people. He did not argue with her when she chose to work in a faraway place for less money because she liked a club's managers and turned down a more lucrative engagement in a place where she had not been treated well. He smoothed the way for her, placed her happiness above financial considerations, treated her as a person not as a property. Looking back, Lena feels that without Ralph and Lennie she would not have been able to continue her career as a black singer in a predominantly white, racially segregated world.

By the time Lena and Lennie had been secretly married for some three years, they had both grown weary of carrying the burden of their secret. The attitudes of Americans toward interracial marriage had not changed at all, but the attitude of the two individuals had. They had come to feel that living openly and normally together was not a privilege they hoped one day to enjoy but a basic, human right that they deserved to have immediately. Being the more well known, and having the opportunity to speak publicly more often, Lena was the one who broke the news. In October 1950, she told Erskine Johnson of the *Los Angeles Daily News,* "We were secretly married in Paris in 1947 . . . We could not have been married in Hollywood at that time, for our own state of California did not permit white people to marry people of any other group."

The story made headlines in some papers, and was carried in most papers across the country. As expected, there was a lot of controversy. Lena and Lennie were criticized by some groups, supported by others. The reaction from both black and white sectors was mixed, but it was strong. Two people in love, and married, were, because they were of different races, open to the pronouncements and opinions of just about everyone. As a result, they spent as much time as they could in Europe, where their marriage was not viewed as so scandalous. They even considered making Europe their home, but they decided not to. They had close family and personal ties in the United States, and besides, they considered the United States their home.

Around the same time as Lena made public her marriage to Lennie Hayton, she also left M-G-M. She was tired of being offered only small singing parts in white musicals: *Words and Music* starring Judy Garland and Gene Kelly, *Till the Clouds Roll By* starring Van Heflin, *Two Girls and a Sailor* starring Van Johnson and June Allyson. In none of these movies was her part important to the story. For *Two Girls and a Sailor* the cast list read "Specialty . . . Lena Horne." In the others, she was a

"Guest Star." Neither M-G-M nor the other big studios were making all-black movies anymore. Even if they had been, she would not have been very interested. She wanted a chance to do dramatic roles. Since she didn't expect any other studio to offer her a contract, she saw no reason to remain in Hollywood. Lennie left M-G-M, too, and they went to New York, the center of the new television industry as well as the country's theatrical hub. Lena hoped to get a chance to do drama in television and on Broadway.

Back in New York, Lena sought to establish a residence in Manhattan, but she and Lennie were not exactly welcomed by prospective landlords. She was black and he was Jewish, and they were married to each other. Any one of these facts would have caused them to be turned away, and they happened to have all three working against them. Lena was particularly dismayed when they were refused an apartment at the Eldorado, a luxury building on Central Park West owned by Bishop C. M. ("Daddy") Grace, a black religious leader.

As if this were not difficult enough, Lena found that she had been "blacklisted" from television. It was the time of the cold war between the western democracies and the communist countries. Many Americans were convinced that the communists were trying to take over the United States, and in the early 1950s a real anti-communist hysteria was sweeping the country. Senator Joseph McCarthy, a Democrat from Wisconsin, was conducting hearings into suspected un-American activities and making daily headlines with his accusations of treason. In this atmosphere, anyone who had ever been a member of the Communist Party, or who had even been associated with people or organizations that the anti-communist "witch hunters" deemed un-American, was suspected. Many very patriotic and completely innocent Americans were ruined during this period.

Entertainers were particular targets of the anti-communists.

Lists of entertainers with suspected communist ties were circulated around the various branches of the entertainment industry. A publication called *Red Channels* was circulated among TV bosses. It contained lists of people who were labeled by a small group of powerful people as "tainted" by communism. Lena was on the list. She was a friend of Paul Robeson, who in his frustration over segregation in his own country had turned to communism. She was also a member of the Council for African Affairs and Hollywood Independent Citizens Committee for the Arts, Sciences, and Professions, which some chose to see as further evidence that she leaned towards communism. These associations were enough to bar her from making television appearances. Like many others who were blacklisted, she was never officially investigated by any government agency, and no formal charges were ever brought against her. But in those days, when Americans were pointing accusing fingers at one another, a mere accusation was enough to get put on one of the many blacklists.

Still free to play the cabaret circuit, Lena and Lennie got as much work as they could in clubs. As often as possible, they traveled outside the country where they were free of the anti-communist hysteria and of the prejudice against them as a mixed couple. One such trip to Europe particularly stands out in Lena's memory. When she sang in Glasgow, Scotland, the audience screamed with enthusiasm. In Stockholm, Sweden, audiences greeted her with hushed respect and covered the stage with flowers. Gail and Teddy traveled with her and Lennie on this trip. Gail took tea with little girls all over Europe, and Teddy became a seasoned traveler. Life in Europe was so free compared to life in the United States that Lena again thought about moving there permanently. Although she did not act on her feelings this time either, it is ironic that in Europe she and Lennie got their first line on their long-sought Manhattan apartment.

In Paris, in 1956, they met José Iturbi, conductor of the Rochester, New York, Symphony Orchestra. He was planning a benefit concert and asked Lena to take part in it. During the negotiations that followed, Lena and Lennie discovered that Iturbi had an apartment in New York that he was not using. In exchange for Lena's agreeing to do the benefit, they asked to take over his lease. He agreed, and three years after they had first started looking, Lena and Lennie had their Manhattan apartment at last.

At about the same time as they got the apartment, Lena found an opportunity to get off the *Red Channels* blacklist. Ed Sullivan wanted her on his television show. He did not believe in blacklisting people from television, and although he could not just bypass the blacklist he had considerable influence in the industry and opened the way for Lena to get her name off the list. Lena had to meet with George Sokolsky, a well-known political columnist. Once again, she had to swallow her pride and beg for permission to work. But she had it easier than many other entertainers, who had to appear before congressional commit-tees in order to clear themselves. For some, getting off the blacklist came too late to salvage their crippled careers. Paul Robeson was one who never recovered from being blacklisted, and it is said that he carried his bitterness over his treatment to the grave.

Once Lena's name was removed from the *Red Channels* blacklist, she enjoyed quite a bit of television work. Her appearance on *The Ed Sullivan Show* led to invitations to perform on Steve Allen's *Tonight Show*, the forerunner of Johnny Carson's show, and on *The Perry Como Show*. She especially enjoyed performing with Como, who disregarded the unspoken rule that blacks and whites must not touch when performing together and acted naturally toward her. This television expo-sure was good for her career, introducing her to audiences that had not seen her perform in nightclubs and in movies. It also brought her more offers to perform in the big nightclubs in New York and Las Vegas and on the West Coast, and she was able to negotiate clauses in her contracts that shielded her from racial problems. By 1957, Lena was an acknowledged star on the club circuit.

But she was also forty years old, and she did not want to be a cabaret singer forever. She hoped her television exposure would lead to other career opportunities.

10
Lena on Broadway

Although she was pleased to be off the *Red Channels* blacklist and able to do television, Lena knew that she could not look to television for more than occasional relief from her grueling life as a cabaret singer. She could not make a living at television work. The only way an entertainer could survive working solely in television was to have his or her own show, and in the late 1950s that was not possible for a black entertainer.

One major network tried to offer a musical variety show with a black host in the late 1950s. Nat King Cole was a very popular singer whose records were bought by both whites and blacks and who got considerable air play on white radio stations. Thus, *The Nat King Cole Show* was aired on a trial basis, with the hope of attracting sponsors. But although the viewing audience was sizable, and the response from midwesterners and easterners was positive, potential sponsors caved in to the demands of the racist South. *The Nat King Cole Show* aired for six weeks without a sponsor, and then it was canceled. This pathetic outcome set the precedent for the almost total absence of blacks on television for years to come.

There were very few blacks on television in any capacity. There were virtually none in the dramatic shows, and certainly none in advertisements. Eddie Anderson, who played Rochester on *The Jack Benny Show*, was for a long time the only black seen regularly on television. It was only on musical variety shows and interview shows with white hosts that blacks appeared very often, and once an entertainer had appeared on all those shows, he or she had to wait quite a long time to be invited back again.

As for variety specials starring blacks, they were completely unheard of and could not attract sponsors. Lena had to go to England to do specials on television. The British Broadcasting Company (BBC) produced two specials starring Lena. The second one was aired for New York audiences, but that was the only place in the country where it was broadcast.

Broadway was a more realistic alternative for Lena, and in fact once she moved to New York she began to receive a large number of scripts and offers to do Broadway shows. But she rejected them all, for a combination of reasons. One factor was money. Going into rehearsal for a Broadway show was a risky affair. She could not afford to keep her musicians on her payroll while she rehearsed. But if the show flopped, she would need to get back on the road right away, and so she would need her musicians. With Gail in college at Radcliffe and Teddy due to enter college soon, she was reluctant to consider doing a show unless she felt its success was almost guaranteed.

Unfortunately, every show she considered that seemed likely to do well on Broadway also required her to play the kind of stereotyped role that she found objectionable. Thus, if she didn't turn down a part because she considered the show too much of a risk, she turned it down because it wasn't the kind of part she wanted to play. Yearning to perform on Broadway, but unwilling to do so under the circumstances that were presented her, she continued to travel the cabaret circuit.

Late in 1956 when she was working at the Waldorf-Astoria

Hotel in New York City, composer Harold Arlen and his partner, lyricist Yip Harburg, came to see her. Lena had been an admirer of Arlen's music ever since the Cotton Club days, when he had composed the music for some of the club's shows. She sang many Arlen songs and included a great deal of his music in her nightclub repertoire. Thus, she was delighted to accept Arlen's invitation to visit his home to hear the music and read the script for a new Broadway show called *Jamaica*.

Arlen and Yarburg had originally written the show for Harry Belafonte, who had helped to introduce the current craze for calypso music and singing. But Belafonte was so busy performing as the top calypso star that he did not have time to do the show that had been written expressly for him. Arlen and Yarburg still wanted to take the show to Broadway, and they believed that Lena Horne, in the major female role, would prove a sufficient drawing card to make the show successful.

Lena loved the music for the show. The script was another matter entirely. The story was about an island fisherman who prefers nature, simplicity, and innocence to the trappings of modern civilization. Unfortunately, Savanna, the girl he loves, does not share his ideas. Savanna has a television set, and it opens up a new world for her. She comes to believe that New York City, as presented on television, is the only place to live, and she refuses to listen to her girlfriend, who warns her that she risks losing a good man.

Lena felt that the character of the fisherman had great depth and substance, the qualities she was looking for in a role. But the character of Savanna seemed shallow and superficial. She felt that the part of Savanna's girlfriend, though less important, was the better female role. But Arlen and Yarburg wanted her to play the female lead. They assured her that they would make changes in the script to give Savanna the depth of character that Lena desired.

Lena thought and thought about whether or not she should

With her husband, Lennie Hayton, in Stockholm, Sweden, August, 1952. *Wide World Photos.*

Lena Horne in *Meet Me in Las Vegas,* 1956. *From the Frank Driggs Collection.*

ena Horne in Paris, May, 1956. *Black Star Photos.*

(Left) In *Jamaica*, 1956. *Theatre Collection, Museum of the City of New York.*

(Below) With Ricardo Montalban in *Jamaica. Theatre Collection, Museum of the City of New York.*

(Above) Laurence Harvey, Janis Paige, Milton Berle, Lena Horne, and Jack Benny, c. 1960. *From the Frank Driggs Collection.*

(Right) With her daughter, Gail Jones, 22, backstage at the New York Playhouse, where Ms. Jones made her stage debut in the musical *Valmouth.* October 7, 1960. *United Press International Photo.*

(Above) Lena Horne at the march on Washington, August 28, 1963. *Ivan Massar, Black Star Photos.*

(Left) Lena Horne, 1960s. *Photo courtesy of Duncan P. Schiedt.*

(Above) With her daughter, Gail Jones Lumet, and her granddaughter Amy, 1981. ©*1981 Adam Scull, Black Star Photos.*

(Below) A cake for Lena on her 64th birthday following a performance of *The Lady and Her Music,* June 30, 1981. *United Press International Photo.*

(Above) With Paul Newman and his wife, Joanne Woodward, after a performance of *The Lady and Her Music*, July 10, 1981. *United Press International Photo.*

(Left) Lena Horne greeting Cab Calloway backstage after a performance of *The Lady and Her Music*, July 10, 1981. *United Press International Photo.*

Filming an "I Love New York" commercial, October, 1981. © *Adam Scull, Black Star Photos.*

Celebrating the first anniversary of the Broadway show. To her left is Dionne Warwick and to her right is Sarah Vaughan. May 12, 1982. *United Press International Photo.*

take the role. She had hoped for a stronger part, but she *had* been assured that the script would be changed. The songs she would sing were wonderful. And a Harold Arlen show with calypso music was almost guaranteed to do well on Broadway. Deciding that her chance to get on the stage was now or never, she accepted the part.

LENA HORNE TO QUIT CLUBS, ENTER THEATER

that was the headline for a story in the *Hollywood Citizen-News* issue of July 2, 1957. Aline Mosby, a correspondent for the paper, reported that as Lena prepared to leave the nightclub circuit for the Broadway theater, droves of people came to the Cocoanut Grove to see her act. Calling Lena "one of the highest paid club acts since 1941," the reporter quoted Lena as saying she did not want to grow old on the cabaret circuit singing songs about love and sex. Lena went on to explain: "I suppose I'll return to clubs now and then so long as I have teeth. But nothing is harder than singing all the time in clubs. I've been in a position recently to choose where I sang here and in Las Vegas, San Francisco and New York. But for many years I put up with rude bosses and unpleasant surroundings.

"One thing I'll miss about nightclubs is the closeness to my audience—you don't get that on Broadway. But I won't miss having to concentrate hard because everybody is loaded and having a ball."

Lena left the cabaret circuit with very few regrets. She had never considered nightclub singing a very respectable career, and her major stardom on that circuit had not changed her opinion. In fact, she considered it a downright lowly occupation compared to acting on Broadway. Unfortunately, when she came to do Broadway stage work, that attitude worked against her. Although she plunged excitedly into rehearsals at first, she soon began to feel totally inadequate as an actress.

Although she had previous Broadway experience, the shows she had appeared in had been primarily variety shows. They had not called for much acting. She'd had acting experience in Hollywood, but acting in films and acting on the stage are very different. In films, one can always count on another "take" if a scene does not go right. On the stage, in front of a live audience, actors do not have that luxury. Although the plot of *Jamaica* was thin at best, for maximum effect the actors had to act; they couldn't just let the musical numbers carry them along. Lena found that she was entirely unprepared for stage acting, and trying to understand the art was exhausting. It seemed to her that those who were responsible for teaching her the craft spoke only in vague generalizations and did not tell her exactly what she had to do. She found the days of rehearsals long, demanding, and often overwhelming. To make matters worse, the part of Savanna was never rewritten to suit her, and playing the role of a character of whom she disapproved and which she felt bordered on a stereotype put her under even greater strain. Often she would arrive home in tears, unable to contain her frustration any longer. Lennie and her children were patient and understanding, and she was reminded again of how fortunate she was to have her loved ones. But even their support was not enough to make her feel that she would ever achieve competence on the stage.

Jamaica was tried out in Boston before being taken to Broadway. It was not well received by the Boston critics, who did not like either the show or Lena's performance. Fortunately, although she suspected the show had not done well in Boston, Lena did not read the reviews herself. Years earlier, producer Lew Leslie had advised her not to read reviews, and she had followed his advice since then. The rest of the cast kept the bad news from her.

Despite the poor reviews in Boston, *Jamaica* continued on to

New York and Broadway as scheduled. For two nights it played to private audiences for the benefit of charity. The people attending paid as much as $100.00 per ticket, and they expected to see a good show. But they were unmoved by Lena's performance, and she sensed the coldness in their polite applause. She reacted by feeling absolutely nothing. She was not upset, she just felt numb. This was hardly the best way for an actress to feel as her show's official opening night approached.

On the evening of November 30, 1957, Lena sat dejectedly in her dressing room waiting for her call. All she could think about was how much her feet hurt. Suddenly, there was a loud knock at the door. She opened it to find a huge bouquet of flowers with a card that said, "Savanna, we love you, The Crew." It was exactly what she needed to revive her spirits, to put her "spunk" back into her.

Her call came. As she made her way to the stage, she remembered what the play's director, Bobby Lewis, had said to her that afternoon: "When you make your entrance tonight, make it like you belong there and stand still." She took her position inside the little shack that was Savanna's home and waited as the opening music began and the curtain rose. Later, she remembered, "The entrance music stopped. I flung those shutters open hard and spoke clearly—like my grandmama taught me—barged down the steps and stood still like Bobby had advised me—and New York treated me like a hometown girl." The audience roared its approval; the applause was deafening, and Lena and the rest of the cast were inspired to give the best, most energetic performance they could.

From that time on, working in *Jamaica* was delightful for Lena. Gone were her insecurities about acting; she relaxed and enjoyed herself. As she performed night after night, she came to realize that her years on the cabaret circuit had had some value after all. They had given her stamina, prepared her to take in stride the small problems that arose in the show and among the cast. No longer did she consider the cabaret circuit and the Broadway stage as complete opposites, one lowly and one exalted. She came to understand that professionalism—commitment, hard work, a willingness to learn, respect for one's coworkers—was the backbone of cabaret, vaudeville, and Broadway stage entertaining alike.

Her pleasure working in *Jamaica* was heightened by the opportunity the show gave her to enjoy a settled home life for a change. She returned to her own home and family every night. They actually had two Christmases in a row together at home. Having steady work in one place also enabled Lena to develop new friendships. She got to know the young people in the cast and developed a great admiration for them. Their dedication to their craft, their willingness to scrimp and save and sacrifice to continue their acting or singing or dancing classes, were inspiring. Even more admirable, in her view, was the way they supported each other, regardless of race. For the young actors and dancers and singers in *Jamaica*, black and white, their shared love for their art was far more important than their differences. Age differences didn't seem to concern them either; they accepted her and supported her and respected her experience. The sense of belonging she felt was one that she had never felt before.

During the run of *Jamaica*, Lena also had the opportunity to meet and get to know another group of young people. They were the sons and daughters of her middle-class black friends in New York. Most of these young people were attending southern colleges, and many of them would soon help to launch the student movement for civil and human rights that began in the South in the 1960s. They were proud of being black and unwilling to accept the discrimination and segregation that their parents had bowed to. Their spirit and their activism encouraged

Lena to become more open in dealing with her own racial identity.

Lena felt that during the 1950s she had grown away from her own people. This was not so much because she had been married to Lennie Hayton as it was because she had gradually moved into the bigger nightclubs, to clubs abroad, to places where most blacks would never have the opportunity to go. As a star, she had come into contact with other stars, almost all of whom were white. The friendships she made were, naturally, among people in her profession and on the same rung of the ladder of her profession, and they did not include many black people. She began to view her life as escapist. She realized that for all of her hardships she had been insulated from much of the anguish of day-to-day life for black people in America. She began to feel guilty about the way she had distanced herself from her race.

As long as her work in *Jamaica* occupied her with happy success, Lena did not have to confront these guilt feelings head-on. She could toy with her guilty feelings without really feeling the need to act on them. But when *Jamaica* closed in the spring of 1959, she felt as if she were a dive-bomber that had crashed. She was deeply depressed. This reaction is normal for an actor in a fairly long-running play; for two years she had known exactly where she was going every day, and for two years she had played to approving, applauding audiences. Now she was no longer on stage and there were no audiences to applaud. There were also no immediate prospects for another Broadway show. She had to go back to the cabaret circuit, but she did not feel like the same Lena Horne who had left that circuit two-and-a-half years earlier. Inside, she had a different sense of her position in the world, and that set her apart from other actors who had just ended successful Broadway runs.

She didn't want to sing about love and sex and heartbreak anymore. She wanted to sing songs that had more meaning—

songs about freedom and dignity and humanity. Her exposure to the activism of young black people had made her feel as if she had not done enough, had not fought hard enough, in the past. Even her attempts to make a difference in Hollywood seemed insufficient. Sure, she had stood up against the Hollywood practice of stereotyping all Negroes, but she had just been doing what Walter White and Count Basie had told her to do: She had been a "good little symbol." But where had it gotten her, and what had she proved? Had she made life better for the average black American? Had she made any meaningful difference? The more she questioned the worth of what she had done in the past, the guiltier she felt for not having done more.

Some months after *Jamaica* closed, one of the young black men who had danced in the show dropped in to see her. He had done very well in the show and in Lena's opinion he was a gifted dancer who should go far. But as they sat talking in Lena's living room, the young man confided that since the play had closed he'd had almost no work. He had gone to Puerto Rico and worked with a white manager who had never paid him his full salary, but he could get no work at all in his own country. Lena, looking at the young man sitting in her living room, knew with a painful awareness that he would have to struggle twice as hard because he was black.

She felt that she ought to have done more to smooth the way for young black people like this dancer. Since she didn't feel she had done enough in the past, she yearned to somehow put things right now—to speak out aggressively about all the injustices that black people suffered. But she was afraid that she would look like a phoney if, at this point, she tried to present herself as a fiery militant. She had acquired a reputation as a moderate person. Although the stands she had taken against racial discrimination had seemed to her to be quite radical for their time, through the inverted telescope of history they didn't seem very radical. She had protested discrimination, but often acquiesced to it. She had refused to play maids, but she had played temptresses and similar roles that were nearly as stereotypical. She had appeared in movies with the knowledge that her scenes would be deleted from the films when they were shown in many theaters. Such a history did not give her the credentials to express openly the depths of her own anger over the racism that plagued America. The young people around her were shouting loud protestations about the treatment of their race, but Lena felt that it was too late to join them.

The guiltier she felt for not having done more, the angrier she got at the society that had not allowed her to do more, and eventually that anger and guilt were bound to erupt. They happened to do so in a public place, the Beverly Hills Luau. It was an evening in 1960, and she and Lennie were there waiting to meet Kay Thompson, the M-G-M vocal coach who was their friend, for drinks. Kay was late and Lennie went to telephone her, leaving Lena alone at the table, which was on the dimly lit, upper level of the restaurant. On the other side of a curtain divider a drunk demanded immediate service, and Lena heard the waiter explain that he would be with the man as soon as he finished serving "Miss Horne's table."

"So what," the drunk yelled. "She's just another nigger. Where is she?"

Lena reacted immediately. She jumped up and, grabbing the lamp from her table, held it to her face, identifying herself to the man in strong language. Then she threw the lamp, glasses, an ashtray, and every other item she could reach, straight at him. One of the objects hit him in the face, and blood streamed down from a cut over his eye. A group of waiters and managers hustled the drunk away at about the same time as Lennie grabbed Lena from behind. What happened? Lennie wanted to know. When Lena told him, he asked if she had managed to hit the racist.

When she told him that one of her missiles had made contact, he smiled.

The *Los Angeles Herald Examiner,* among numerous other newspapers, reported the incident on Wednesday, February 17, 1960:

LENA HORNE, FOE TELL OF CAFE ROW

When entertainer Lena Horne learned today that the man she bopped with an ash tray for "making anti-Negro remarks" may sue her, she shrugged: "I'm sorry if he feels that way. I could also sue him for defamation of character."

Miss Horne's target, Harvey St. Vincent, 30, vice-president of an engineering firm, said through attorney William Hays that his future action in the matter had not been decided.

St. Vincent, of 11725 Sunset Blvd., denied making any disparaging remarks about either Miss Horne or her race. The donnybrook shattered the midnight calm of the Luau Restaurant in Beverly Hills early yesterday.

Everyone seems to agree that Miss Horne jumped up from her table and began throwing strikes at St. Vincent, who was seated at an adjoining table.

Don Viray, manager of the plush Polynesian-style restaurant, said a bamboo divider and a model ship separating the two tables may have hampered Miss Horne's aim and saved St. Vincent some lumps.

St. Vincent said he had remarked to a dinner companion that "there is an attractive colored girl sitting at the bar" but that he was not talking about Miss Horne.

"I didn't know she was in the restaurant until I became aware of an attractive woman in a white turban standing over my table raging," he said.

"I asked, 'What's the matter with you?' and that started something."

Miss Horne's recollection of events leading up to the battle was pointedly different.

"He mentioned my name a few times," she said. "His remarks were obviously anti-Negro. In my anger, I started throwing things. I'm glad I didn't hurt him seriously."

Her husband, musical director Lennie Hayton, was an interested but silent spectator as his wife went back over the fight. He had left their table to make a phone call when the outburst occurred.

"When it was all over (St. Vincent was hit in the eye by a conch shell ash tray and prudently withdrew to another table) I sat there and tried to get un-angry," she smiled. "Several other patrons came over and were very apologetic about the whole incident."

Witnesses to the incident said Miss Horne told St. Vincent, "I can hear you. You can't say things like that. This is America, after all."

Beverly Hills police officers who investigated said St. Vincent had admitted making "anti-Negro remarks."

Lena's blowup in the Luau was reported in papers across the country, and she was flooded with mail. The vast majority of it was supportive and came from black people who praised her courageous action. At last, Lena realized that black people wanted to identify with her as much as she wanted to identify with them. She was not "too different" ever to be really accepted by them; they did not dismiss most of her public actions against racism as mere "publicity stunts."

Shortly after the incident, Lena and Lennie took a vacation in the Caribbean, and there, too, countless blacks approached her to congratulate her and thank her for what she had done. She was pleased that the story had been picked up by the international press and glad that elsewhere in the world her people thought of her as one of them. All this positive feedback from black people made her feel even more eager to close the enormous gap that had separated her from most other black people for much of her life.

Around that time, Jean Noble, President of Delta Sigma Theta, a black service sorority, succeeded in contacting her. Noble had sent her letters offering her honorary membership while Lena was working in *Jamaica*, but Lena had developed an aversion to reading her mail over the years because it was so often hate mail. She had not even seen the letters. Jean Noble persisted, and eventually she reached Lena.

Lena did not know very much about DST, and when she learned that it was a sorority her first reaction was negative. Lena remembered sororities from the time she was a teenager in Brooklyn; she thought that they were no more than social groups interested in frivolous activities. During her time as a band singer, she had come to feel that sororities were for privileged people and had little serious meaning. Her only contact with them was when they hired the bands she worked with for parties. Jean Noble explained that DST was different. It was a service-oriented group with over thirty-five thousand members, all of whom were black women college graduates. Delta had the oldest job opportunities program for black women in the country; it gave scholarships and worked with African women; members were also active in voter-registration drives. Lena realized that Delta Sigma Theta represented that kind of social activism that her grandmother had been so committed to, and she was proud to accept honorary membership and to be associated with DST. Thereafter, the sorority became an important point of contact for her. When she was on the road she would meet its members, all black women—teachers, doctors, lawyers, housewives. Being part of DST, as they were, reaffirmed her position as one of them—a concerned black woman. They confirmed to her that she was not "different" racially but only in the nature of her experience, and they also helped her to identify more closely with the tradition of her grandmother. She liked their ethic of hard work and sacrifice and doing something to make the world better. She often says that if she'd had her own way, she would have gone to college and become a schoolteacher in some small, quiet community. If she had pursued that course, she probably would have joined DST, and she found it somehow fitting to have become part of the sorority, although in a very roundabout way.

Through her association with Delta Sigma Theta, Lena became involved with the National Council of Negro Women, founded by Mary McLeod Bethune, another close friend of Cora Calhoun Horne's. Ms. Bethune, an outstanding Negro woman scholar, was the founder of a normal school for teachers now called Bethune-Cookman College in Daytona Beach, Florida. She was also a confidante of Mrs. Eleanor Roosevelt, and the two women met often to discuss the problems of blacks and women in the United States. Lena admired Ms. Bethune and again felt proud of the work women like her had been doing for so many years.

These new friendships were very satisfying to Lena; so were the renewed connections she felt to her family past. They all seemed to happen around the same time, and often Lena marveled at the coincidence. At other times, it occurred to her that the women of DST and the National Council of Negro Women, women like Mary McLeod Bethune and Jean Noble, had been there all along, but that she had not been open to them before.

11
Civil Rights Activist

In the spring of 1963, Jean Noble, with whom Lena had become quite friendly, asked her to take part in a Mother's Day march in Birmingham, Alabama. This was to be no ordinary Mother's Day march but a march in protest against segregation in Birmingham. It was just one of many protests that were taking place in the South at this time. Beginning with the Montgomery bus boycott in another Alabama city in the late 1950s, the Civil Rights Movement had been born. In 1960 black southern college students had launched a movement of their own by sitting in at segregated store lunch counters. From there, movements arose spontaneously in many other parts of the South. The Southern Christian Leadership Conference—a group of black ministers that included Dr. Martin Luther King, Jr.—the Student Nonviolent Coordinating Committee, and other organizations like the NAACP and CORE (Congress of Racial Equality) were working sometimes independently and sometimes in cooperation with each other to boycott businesses that discriminated against blacks, to protest segregation laws and practices, and to conduct drives to register blacks to vote. White resistance to the civil rights movement was determined and ugly, and the protestors and marchers and voter-registration workers had suffered arrests and beatings and fear campaigns. But their ranks continued to grow.

Lena was excited and challenged by the movement. At last, blacks in large numbers were saying, "No, we will not bow to segregation any more." And what was even more admirable was that they were protesting nonviolently. Under the direction of Dr. Martin Luther King, Jr., the protesters were suffering white violence without physically fighting back. The philosophy of nonviolence is that words and passive resistance, if used properly, can be powerful weapons, and the civil rights movement was attracting considerable sympathy around the world.

Birmingham had been selected by Dr. King and other leaders of the movement as a target city, and a massive protest was planned. Members of Delta Sigma Theta were to take part in the Mother's Day march, and Lena was to sing on the steps of a church, urging the marchers on. Unfortunately, Jean Noble's invitation came just a couple of days before the march. Lena and Lennie were in Palm Springs, California, where they had purchased a small house in the late 1950s. It was too far away from Birmingham for Lena to get there in time by train, and she did not care to fly. Ever since the time when she had flown around the country entertaining troops, and had been in several near-crashes, Lena had had an aversion to flying. She traveled by airplane only in emergencies, and although she would have liked to participate in the Birmingham march, she did not feel it was crucial for her to be there.

But the real reason she did not go was fear of violence. In earlier marches, Birmingham firemen had turned their hoses on full upon the marchers, and the police had turned their dogs on the victims of the ripping blasts. Television cameras recorded every detail, and Lena and millions of other Americans had watched in horror. As deeply as she wanted to help the civil rights cause, Lena was not ready to put her life in danger. She felt very guilty for refusing to attend the march.

That same evening, Lena received a telephone call from James Baldwin, a prominent black writer who had written movingly about conditions for blacks in the South. Lena had met Baldwin when he had come backstage during *Jamaica*'s run to visit some of his friends who were in the cast. She had also written him a fan letter, after reading some of his work, for she admired his brilliance and his writing. But she was still astonished to hear from him.

Baldwin explained that he had been contacted by Attorney General Robert Kennedy, who was concerned about the violence against blacks such as had taken place in Birmingham. Kennedy wanted to meet with some prominent blacks to discuss the situation, and Baldwin felt that Lena should participate in the meeting. Lena was reluctant; she didn't want to be trotted out as a symbol again, she wanted to respond to the crisis as an individual, not as a "prominent black."

Later the same night, Jean Noble called to tell Lena that the DST women had never gotten a chance to march, because of the violence. Lena told her about Baldwin's call, and Jean Noble urged her to accept his invitation. Lena remained unconvinced until Lennie persuaded her that it was her responsibility to do whatever she could to help stop the violence they had watched with such horror on television.

The hastily called meeting was set for New York, and Lena had to fly. The gathering, which took place at an apartment belonging to one of the Kennedys, included Lorraine Hansberry, the late playwright and author of *A Raisin in the Sun;* Rip Torn, the actor, who was also a southerner and a friend of James Baldwin's; Harry Belafonte; Dr. Kenneth Clark, the famous black sociologist; Jerome Smith, a young man from the Student Nonviolent Coordinating Committee; Robert Kennedy and his aide, Burke Marshall; James Baldwin; and Lena.

As the meeting opened, Dr. Clark presented a list of statistics that showed the overwhelming lack of opportunities for blacks in education, employment, housing, voting, and other essential human rights. In response, Robert Kennedy seemed to Lena to be defensive. He tried to persuade the group that he and his brother, President John F. Kennedy, were doing all they could for blacks and that it was more than any previous administration had done. Lena and most of the other members of the group did not hesitate to commend the Kennedys for the tough stand they had taken to protect James Meredith as he tried to become the first black to enroll at the University of Mississippi in 1962; President Kennedy had assigned U. S. marshals to escort him. They agreed that such major changes required time, and they might have been persuaded that the Kennedy best was indeed all they could expect if Jerome Smith had not taken strong exception to the generally conciliatory tone of the others. Smith was working on voter-registration drives in the South, and he had seen and experienced the violent white reaction to the attempts to gain for blacks the most basic right of Americans. He and his family had been threatened and he had been forced to send his wife and children away for their own protection. He had been jailed and severely beaten, and he showed his scars for all to see. He was in no mood to be conciliatory; he seethed with fury.

Lena recalled, "You could not encompass his anger, his fury, in a set of statistics, nor could Mr. Belafonte and Dr. Clark and Miss Horne, the fortunate Negroes, who had never been in a southern jail keep up the pretense of being the mature, responsible spokesmen for the race anymore. All of a sudden the fancy phrases like 'depressed area' and 'power structure' and all the rest were nothing. It seemed to me that this boy just put it like it was. He communicated the plain, basic suffering of being a Negro. The primeval memory of everyone in that room went to work after that. We all went back to nitty-gritty with that kid who was out there in cotton patches trying to get poor, miserable Negro people not to be scared to sign their names to a piece of paper saying they'd vote. We were back at the level where a man just wants to be a man, living and breathing, where, unless he has the right all the rest is only talk."

Everyone was caught off-guard by Smith's raw anger and his passionate recital of his own experience. By this time, the United States was involved in the Vietnam War and young Americans Smith's age were being drafted to fight over there. James Baldwin asked Smith if he would be willing to go to Vietnam and fight for his country, and Smith responded with an emphatic, "No!" Although he risked his life daily in Mississippi, he was adamantly opposed to risking it in Vietnam so long as Mississippi was permitted to exist as it did. Robert Kennedy was perplexed; he did not understand Smith's feelings. But the blacks at the meeting did. Jerome Smith forced them to take a militant position, too. They moved to impress upon Robert Kennedy the seriousness of the situation in the South and warned him that full-scale war was likely to erupt if the government did not step in.

Lena returned home from the meeting troubled and guilt-ridden once again. She felt she had to do something. She called the NAACP and told them that she wanted to go South, and the organization arranged for her to sing at a rally in Jackson, Mississippi. Having gotten her wish, Lena now worried about how southern blacks would receive her. She felt that by now she was an overused, overworked symbol of another time; she regretted that she had not been more militant in the past. She tried to imagine how black southerners would respond to her, a northern, privileged black. She felt that they would be justified in not welcoming her. But she felt she had to go. Jean Noble agreed with her, and Billy Strayhorn, her old friend, said he would play for her.

Lena, Billy, and Jean arrived in Jackson together and were met by Medgar Evers, an NAACP field representative who ran the organization's office in Jackson. He explained that he would like to have had them stay at his home, but his home had recently been bombed and had not yet been repaired. He and his family remained in the badly damaged house and Medgar continued with his NAACP activities. Lena was deeply impressed and permanently inspired by the strength and dedication of Medgar Evers. At the risk of his own life, and the safety of his family, he worked tirelessly to inspire black people in the Jackson area to demand their rights.

Dick Gregory, the comedian turned social activist, was flying in and out of Jackson and other parts of the South at this time. Gregory was another person for whom Lena had great respect. He had left a lucrative nightclub career to face physical abuse, jail, and the hard, dangerous work of civil rights activism in the South. Gregory was in Jackson for the rally, and following it he wanted to take an angry protest march to the streets of Jackson. The NAACP, which had organized the rally, disagreed with Gregory's idea; and Medgar Evers was ordered not to go into the streets but to keep the protest confined to the rally. Angered, Gregory accused the NAACP of limiting the protest to the rally because they wanted to protect Lena.

Lena did not like the suggestion that she was getting special treatment. It was a reminder that she always felt ordinary blacks thought her too "different." She wondered if the people at the rally would feel as Gregory did and boo her; she expected the worst from the southern black protesters. But she had underestimated the people at the rally. They cheered her, and appreciated her coming to Jackson to lend her support. She left Jackson feeling that they had given her a lot more than she had given them.

Hugh Downs of NBC's *Today Show* invited Lena to appear on the show shortly after she returned to New York from Mississippi. Lena was emotionally charged from her experience in the South and eager to share her feelings with the television audience. Since she had to be at the NBC building by 6:00 A.M. and since she was tired from all the traveling she had been doing, she went to bed early the night before. The next morning, as she sat in the cramped waiting area drinking coffee and waiting for her turn on the air, she was informed by a floor manager that her appearance was being delayed until Roy Wilkins arrived. Wilkins had replaced Walter White as national president of the NAACP, and Lena was pleased to hear that she would be sharing the air with him. Then the floor manager said that Wilkins had probably been delayed because of the previous night's tragedy. Lena wanted to know what he meant. He told her that while she was sleeping the night before, Medgar Evers had been blasted in the back with a double-barreled shotgun near the back door of his home.

It had been less than a week since Lena had been with Medgar Evers, and she became hysterical. But when Roy Wilkins arrived, she managed to pull herself together and went before the cameras to try to share with the audience the misery of the senseless killing.

At a luncheon in honor of Dr. Martin Luther King, Jr., later that day, Medgar Evers's death dominated the affair. All Lena could think of was that when they killed Medgar his white murderers had tried to kill what he stood for. She hoped that his courage would live on in the minds of the people he had left behind and that he had not died for nothing. The Reverend King invited Lena to go to Atlanta to sing at a Southern Christian Leadership Conference (SCLC) rally, and she agreed. Mercer

Ellington, Duke Ellington's son, would conduct for her. But at
this massive rally, Lena did not find the same inspiration as she
had in Jackson, Mississippi, at the rally organized by Medgar
Evers. For Lena, the Jackson rally with Medgar was the apex of
the civil rights movement.

During the summer of 1963, Lena went through a period of
self-examination, trying to find and understand her own place in
the black struggle for civil and human rights. She did not want to
be a mere symbol; she wanted to take an active part in the
movement. But if she tried to be like Dick Gregory, fasting and
allowing herself to be arrested and jailed, she knew she would
not be honest, and she knew, too, that no one else would take
her seriously. So, she did what felt "right" for her.

In the historic march on Washington by civil rights groups on
August 28, 1963, she marched with the Deltas. Some of those
who marched were elderly women who had marched in the first
suffragette parade to demand voting rights for women, and being
with them made Lena feel part of a long line of concerned and
activist women. She continued to sing at rallies and benefits, but
began to sing songs that were not in her usual repertoire, songs
that reflected her feelings about what was happening in her
country.

In the fall of 1963 Lena was asked to do a benefit at Carnegie
Hall for SNCC. Frank Sinatra had agreed to do the show as well,
providing that the proceeds from the second night of the two-
night show would go to a charity he supported. Lena wanted a
special song to sing at the benefit, and Harold Arlen and Yip
Harburg teamed up to produce "Silent Spring" for her, a song
that was dedicated to the four young black children who were
killed when their church in Birmingham was bombed by racist
whites on September 15, 1963. Another musical team, lyricists
Betty Comden and Adolph Green, wrote new lyrics for the
Jewish song "Hava Nagillah" and created a song called "Now"
for Lena to sing at the benefit.

Because SNCC was a very militant organization, tickets to the benefit did not sell well at first. Lena got out and stomped the pavement, called her friends, talked up the show until all the tickets were sold. In this case, she was glad to be a symbol, for it gave her influence to get accomplished something she really believed in.

Both "Silent Spring" and "Now" were very well received at the Carnegie Hall benefit, and Lena later recorded "Now." The lyrics were so militant that some radio stations banned it from the air, but in spite of this the song became a hit, a best seller, and Lena was pleased to be able to get her message out to the people.

By the fall of 1963, Lena was speaking her mind in a clear, determined fashion when she was interviewed by reporters. In the past, she had tended to soft-pedal her remarks about discrimination and about American society. Although, on occasion, she had spoken out about particular issues or incidents, she had kept to herself the cumulative effect of racism on her personality and her career. In late September, the *Los Angeles Times* carried an interview with her under the headline LENA HORNE TELLS WHAT IT'S LIKE TO BE A NEGRO, and in it Lena told how she had developed "guile" and "toughness" in order to avoid breaking under the pressures of white racism. She told about how M-G-M had limited her film career due to racism. She recalled many of her experiences with racism during her years in Hollywood and the regular letters from Walter White of the NAACP reminding her of her "position" there. About her family, she said, "I came from what was called one of the first families of Brooklyn. It was a family that never talked about the fact that we were all descendants of slave women. Yet it was the rape of slave women by their masters which accounted for our white blood which, in turn, made us Negro 'Society.' "

Lena had never been so open with a reporter about her feelings, and she felt good about opening up at last and telling the public how she really felt. Of course, she also realized that she could not have done so twenty years earlier without risking her career. The racial climate in America had begun to change, and although there was still much improvement needed, Lena felt optimistic.

Other changes took place in Lena's life in 1963. That was the year that her daughter, Gail, married the director Sidney Lumet, a white man. Lena found it hard to accept the marriage, not because her daughter had married a white man but because she was losing Gail. Having recently graduated from Radcliffe, Gail had returned to New York to live with her mother and Lennie, and Lena had looked forward to being a real mother to Gail. During so many of Gail's growing up years, Lena had felt guilty about not being a proper mother and being away on the road so much. She had determined to make it up to Gail once she finished college and came home to live, and now Gail was depriving her of that chance by marrying and moving away. It seemed cruel and unfair to Lena that this would happen just when they had a chance to be together. Gail and her new husband moved to London, and their first child was born there in 1964. Lena flew to London to be with her daughter. Ironically, Gail's pregnancy was as difficult as Lena's first pregnancy (with Gail) had been, and during the hours when both mother's and baby's lives were in danger, Lena realized she had been selfish to want her daughter to stay with her and help her assuage her own guilt. Both Gail Lumet and her new baby, Amy, survived the crisis, and from that time on Lena supported her daughter's marriage and acted like a typical grandmother toward Amy.

Around the same time, Lena also strengthened her ties with her father. Although he had stopped speaking to her for a time after her marriage to Lennie Hayton, Teddy Horne had eventually come around and accepted the marriage for his daughter's sake. When Lena had bought a small hotel in Las Vegas, she had asked her father to run it, and it was there that she reached him one day when, on impulse, she called him to tell him how much he meant to her.

She had been thinking about him a lot, and she called to tell him that she had just realized that she had been identifying with his independent spirit all her life, without knowing it. He understood what she was talking about immediately and assured her, "You've got nothing to apologize for." Overcome by emotion, Lena told her father that she loved him—a milestone for her, since she had always believed that to admit love was to admit weakness.

Thus, Lena completed her spiritual reconnection with the Horne line. Over the years she had come to respect her grandmother, and now she had been able to admit her identification with her father. She had reached a considerable amount of self-understanding in this way. But there were still pieces of her past that she could not make fit. She still felt that it would take the rest of her life to understand her mother; and she wondered if she and her son, Teddy, would ever have a satisfying relationship. Teddy had spent most of his life with Louis, and he and his mother were not close. Lena still felt great guilt over having failed Teddy, but now he was a young man, and she wondered if she would ever have the chance to make it up to him.

12

Tragedy and Renewal

Although Lena marks 1963 as her year of self-realization, when she decided that she no longer wanted to spend her time singing in high-priced nightclubs for predominantly white audiences, she spent two more years on the club circuit, trying to balance that career with her work in the civil rights movement. It took her this much time to emerge from the shell of the old Lena into the new Lena. During this time, she felt considerable conflict about her dual life, and by 1965 she felt strong enough to quit the club circuit almost entirely in order to devote her full time to her work with Delta and the National Council of Negro Women. She exchanged singing tours for speaking tours, traveling the country to lecture under the auspices of the National Council of Negro Women. At first, she wondered if she had a right to speak to black people about how they could go about changing their lives by speaking up for their rights, but she discovered that she was well-received wherever she went and that her audiences were greatly inspired by her personal determination.

Her absence from the club circuit made her all the more sought after, and during this time she received many lucrative offers from producers, promoters, and club owners. But with very few exceptions, Lena turned them down. She'd had enough cabaret singing to last the rest of her life. If someone had approached her to do a television special, or a movie, she would have felt differently, but there were no such offers. Television, and Hollywood, were still not ready for the new Lena Horne, nor probably even for the old Lena Horne. But Lena Horne was ready for television and the movies. She realized that through these media she could reach many more people than the select audiences who could see her at clubs; one needn't be white and well-to-do to have a TV or buy a ticket for a movie.

At last, in 1967, Lena Horne had a television special produced in the United States. *Monsanto Night Presents Lena Horne* aired on NBC. Wayne Warga, a *New York Times* staff writer, asked Lena why it had taken so long for her to appear in an American television special:

"Isn't that weird?" she responded. "I don't know why, other than to say that both you and I know damn well why. Even Harry Belafonte's first shows came from the BBC. They were all made before the breakthrough [of blacks into television]. It's been very slow. I'm amazed I've had to wait this long."

Nevertheless, she confessed to Warga, she was somewhat relieved that for once she was not scoring a first. Harry Belafonte and the Supremes, among other black entertainers, had already had American specials.

Lena's special featured the popular black singer O. C. Smith, who at that time had a hit record called "Little Green Apples," and David Janssen, the white star of a hit TV series called *The Fugitive*. But most of it was Lena. Although she did duets with her guests, she also sang fourteen solos, and they included only three of her traditional songs: "Stormy Weather," "The Surrey with the Fringe on Top," and "Hello, Young Lovers." The others ranged from the Beatles' "Black Bird" to Jimmy Webb's "Didn't We." She also danced.

On the night her special aired, Lena was not at home watching. She was onstage in the midst of a three-week run at Caesar's Palace in Las Vegas with Harry Belafonte. It was her first club appearance since she had done four weeks at the Sands Hotel in Las Vegas the previous year, and she had agreed to do it only because of her friendship with Belafonte. Her general attitude about club work was, "Who needs it?"

Following the special, she did a *Dean Martin Show* and two *Kraft Music Hall* shows almost back to back. But after that, she concentrated on the upcoming Christmas season and spending time with her family, which by now included four grandchildren. Teddy had married and had two children, and Gail had had another child. Lena preferred to read and spend time with her family, and to pursue her activities with Delta and the National Council of Negro Women to singing in clubs. She was fifty years old and she had been working since she was sixteen. People were beginning to remark incredulously about her youthful appearance and wonder if she could really be fifty, but Lena felt every one of her fifty years when she contemplated going back to the club stage. She just didn't feel like going through the hassle.

There was one area of her career, however, that she did not consider "finished," and that was her career in movies. She had never played a dramatic role in a film and had not appeared in any movies since 1956 when she had returned to M-G-M for a small "guest star" part in *Meet Me in Las Vegas* starring Dan Dailey and Cyd Charisse. Thus, when she was approached about appearing in *Death of a Gunfighter* with Richard Widmark, a white star, she was interested. It was a dramatic role, that of a turn-of-the-century madam who ran one of the two houses of prostitution in a small western town. Richard Widmark was the town sheriff and the two were in love. Near the end of the film they got married. The script avoided any mention of color. In this story, Lena could simply play the role of a woman in love with a man.

If the script and the role were not enough to persuade Lena to come out of semiretirement, the idea of being back in California did. Teddy was in California, and Lena desperately wanted to get to know her son better. Teddy, who was in his late twenties by now, was working with the people of Watts, the black ghetto in Los Angeles. Lena was proud of his activism, his concern for his people, and she found it remarkable that he should carry on the tradition of social activism of her family. Equally remarkable was his resemblance to his grandfather and namesake, Teddy Horne; in photographs, the younger Teddy looked just like his grandfather when he was a young man. Lena took very little time to accept the movie offer.

Lena was thrilled to be back in a Hollywood studio. It was nearly thirty years since she had signed her first contract with M-G-M, and there had been many changes in the film industry. The equipment was different, the procedures were different, even the makeup was different. But Lena did not worry about having to adapt to Hollywood movie-making, 1960s style. She had never felt more relaxed. At long last, she felt she had nothing to prove, and so she enjoyed her Hollywood experience. She especially enjoyed recognizing all the big Hollywood stars as they went about their work. Some of these stars were amused that she did not consider herself a star and did not notice that there were just as many people who recognized her and felt privileged to be in her presence. Playing her first dramatic role in a movie did not worry her. Using her experience on Broadway in *Jamaica*, and aware of the lesson she had learned in the musical that professionalism crossed all entertainment-form lines, she worked hard and was willing to take the advice of those around her. When the movie was released, it was critically well received. Kevin Thomas, a staff writer for the *Los Angeles Times*, called it "an engrossing western of considerable intelligence and pertinence," and he described as "admirable" the performances of Lena Horne and Richard Widmark. The fact that she was black and Widmark was white occasioned little comment from the critics, and Lena marveled at the changes that had occurred in American society since the times she had first arrived in Hollywood, when it was taboo for blacks and whites even to touch on film.

As she had hoped, Lena and her son, Teddy, spent a great deal of time together while she was working on *Death of a Gunfighter*. They came to understand each other in ways that had not been possible before, when they saw each other so rarely. Lena was able to talk freely with her son about her decision to leave his father and about her guilt about not taking him with her. Teddy was able to express his honest feelings about the past, too. Lena found her son to be a warm, insightful young man, and she was grateful for the opportunity to become close to him at last. It was one of the happiest times of her life, for during her stay in California she not only made a motion picture in which race was not a factor but also got her son back. Later, she would look back on it as a period of soothing that prepared her in a way for the hard times she would soon have to face.

Not long after Lena completed filming on *Death of a Gunfighter*, her father died. She took it very hard. It had been only a few years since she had come to understand her father, and herself, and had been able to express her love for him openly. Then, within a few months after the elder Teddy's death, Lena's son, Teddy, died of an incurable kidney disease. He was only twenty-nine years old, and his death was particularly hard for Lena to deal with. Her only comfort was that she had become close to Teddy before his death, just as she had with her father before his. Her grief would have been unbearable if she had felt she'd had unfinished business with these two important men in her life.

The third important man in her life, her husband, Lennie, stood by her during this time and gave her the support she needed. During the many months that she mourned the loss of her father and her son, Lennie was there, comforting her. They had been married some twenty-three years by now, and they had one of the most durable marriages started in Hollywood, where they had first met. Although many people still did not approve of interracial marriages, Lena and Lennie had gradually been accepted by the majority of the American public, who realized that such a long-standing marriage was due respect. Thus, it was almost more than Lena could bear when Lennie died, too. In 1971, just a little over a year after her son's death, and nearly eighteen months after her father's death, Lena also lost her husband.

Lena felt as if she was going down, down, down in a whirlpool of grief. She could not handle so much loss coming in such a short time. She went into seclusion, refused to see friends, found it a supreme effort even to get up in the morning. She didn't want to see people anymore, didn't want to sing anymore, didn't want to perform anymore. In fact, she didn't see much use in living anymore. Having lost the three most important men in her life, Lena believed that at the age of fifty-four she, too, had come to an end, and she saw no reason to continue.

Her friends worried about her, and her daughter, Gail, worried about her. But their concern did not seem to penetrate the wall of grief that Lena had constructed around herself. Finally, one friend decided that sympathy and concern were not what Lena needed. She needed to be challenged, she needed to have the survivor in her awakened. The friend visited Lena and demanded, "You can't just sit here for the rest of your life. Get out, get out, get out, and do what you know how to do. Sing."

Somehow, the urgency of her friend's advice penetrated the

layers of grief around Lena. It made her think about her situation in a different way. She began to realize that her father, her son, and her husband would have felt the same way as her friend. She thought about who they had been, how they had lived, and what they had expected from her, and she knew that they would not have wanted her to remain in a pit of sorrow. She began to understand that their memories, their worth as human beings could only be expressed and honored when she demonstrated the strength and character to go on. Lena began to pull herself together, and when she felt capable of facing the outside world again she did indeed face it with what she knew how to do best: She returned singing.

Three years after Lennie's death, Lena went on a British tour with white veteran singer and performer Tony Bennett. They kicked off the tour with a British television special, then traveled throughout Britain singing in concert. Lena had never before toured with another singer, and certainly not a white man, but she thoroughly enjoyed touring with Bennett. He was a consummate professional, and they were able to work together without feeling the competitiveness that often spoils attempts at cooperation between two majors stars.

After their British tour ended, they returned to North America to play in major theaters across the United States and Canada. There were no problems finding accommodations—no hotel management would risk turning away a star of the caliber of Lena Horne—but when Lena did not want to play in Boston because of the hostile racial atmosphere there, Tony bowed to her wishes. They were scheduled to play in Boston at the same time as angry white parents were violently protesting school integration by cross-district busing. Lena refused to go to Boston, and Tony went along with her decision, even though it cost them thousands of dollars.

They began their North American tour in New York, appearing on Broadway on October 30, 1974, to rave reviews. Negotiations to take the show to the Shubert Theater in Los Angeles began immediately, but Lena and Tony left the matter to their agents and continued on with their tour. On Friday, November 1st, they were in Toronto, Ontario, Canada, singing to a standing-room-only crowd who gave Lena a resounding, standing ovation after she completed her fifty-minute segment of the show. Relaxing in her dressing room while Tony entertained the audience, Lena told a reporter that she really didn't understand why the white singer was interested in an "old black broad like me." What she never seemed to be able to realize was that Tony Bennett was also benefitting from touring with Lena. The public knew about the tragedies she had suffered, and Lena had taken on a new quality, an unfathomable depth, that her audiences wanted to experience and perhaps thereby to understand. When she sang a song like Paul Williams's "Loneliness," they realized that she sang it from the experience of her own personal traumas. And when, at the end of her performance, she sang "Stormy Weather," they understood that she was a survivor not just of personal tragedy but of the tragedy of racism in America over the past decades. By the time she and Tony Bennett wound up their tour in Los Angeles, there was no question but that it had been a triumph.

More important to Lena than the professional triumph was the personal triumph. Throughout the tour, she had continued to think about her father, and her son, and her husband. When they had died so close together, she had been nearly shocked into oblivion. But while on tour she had felt closer to them than she had been able to feel since their deaths. She felt her father's protection, just as she had since she had been sixteen and "jail bait" at the Cotton Club. She felt her son's simple concern for other people and her own satisfaction that somehow, despite her lack of contact with him for so many years, he had turned out to be such a good person. She felt Lennie's musical knowledge, his ideas of what arrangements were best for her voice, and his unquestioning support of her. She was able to say, "I was very lucky to have three men who taught me so much."

Lena could see that these three men had given her far more strength than she had imagined she could have. She also realized that her pain and grief had opened her up, made her feel more, made her even more capable of loving, and therefore able to be closer to her audiences. For the first time in her life she started to see her audiences as people, to allow them to feel for her, to embrace them as fellow human beings, and they responded with a love she had never felt from audiences before.

Sometimes, Lena just had to sit back and think about it all. She had gone through so many changes in the past decade or so. Before the late 1950s, she had accomplished more than most people; not only had she become a star but she had surmounted tremendous obstacles and broken down many barriers. But in the last fifteen years or so she had managed to surmount personal obstacles and barriers, and these were the more satisfying successes. She had gotten involved in the civil rights movement and transcended her own old limitations about race. She had made her own peace with her past and with those family members whom she had not seen regularly. And, ironically, with the deaths of her father and son and husband, she had come to understand love in the larger sense of love for her fellow human beings. With the end of her tour with Tony Bennett, she was eager to grow more—professionally and personally. She had spent years hating and resenting her life as a singer on the road; now she found it the most satisfying experience she could ask for. She'd found herself opening, like a bud into a blossom, on that tour; she wanted to have the experience of full flowering.

In 1969, Lena went back onstage alone. Ralph Harris, who had taken over as her road manager soon after her marriage, was still with her as her personal manager. Sherman Sneed, a black man, took over as her road manager. Both men were her friends, and with their assistance Lena was able to resume her work with energy and a sense of being simply who she was. Prior to Lennie's death, she had not ever had complete self-assurance as a singer. She had relied upon his confidence in her, and his arrangements. But by 1975 she could say, "At last, I've made peace with myself and can now stand to hear some of the things I do. I've learned a lot in the craft and I've quit wanting to commit suicide because of not being able to sound like Aretha Franklin, whom I adore, or Dionne Warwick."

She had no idea how much someone like Dionne Warwick admired her. Once, when Lena opened with Billy Eckstine at the Circle Star Theater in the San Francisco Bay area, Dionne Warwick, Lola Falana, and Mary Wilson got together and presented her with a ring. They told Lena that the ring symbolized their feelings for her as a mother figure, as one who had made their own careers possible. "While you're still alive, we want you to know this," they said. They understood the price that Lena had paid for her success and the road she had paved for them. Lena, for her part, took the gesture in the spirit in which it was meant. The assumption on the part of these much younger women that she had one foot in the grave . . . well, she let that pass.

Although she was approaching age sixty, Lena neither looked nor acted it. By 1975 she was working an average of twenty weeks per year. She had given up the Palm Springs house. Lennie had loved the peace and quiet there, but she found it dull. She preferred her New York apartment, where she could be close to Gail and her grandchildren. She was especially glad to have New York as a base when Gail's marriage to Sidney Lumet failed and the couple were divorced. Lena comforted her daughter and gave her all the help she could through that difficult process.

Ironically, while she was comforting Gail, Lena was also

working with Sidney. He directed the movie version of *The Wiz* in which Lena played Glinda the Good Witch. The movie, which was produced by Motown Productions and starred Diana Ross as Dorothy and Michael Jackson as the Tin Man, was released in 1978, the same year in which Gail and Sidney were divorced, but both Sidney Lumet and Lena Horne were professionals and did not allow personal problems to intrude upon their work in the film. Lena enjoyed working on the film, found Diana Ross to be "as sweet as pie," and was pleased by the open admiration of Berry Gordy, the president of Motown. Diana Ross told her that after Berry Gordy saw the daily rushes of Lena's scenes, he told Diana that she had better get her act together because Lena had "sung this song." Although the film received mixed reviews and did not do well at the box office, Lena's performance got rave reviews from many critics, who said that she had stolen Diana Ross's thunder. Lena wished that the film itself had gotten the raves. It had been a very expensive movie, and its poor showing at the box office did not augur well for future high-budget black films.

13

Lena Horne: Legend

B*y the late* 1970s, the era that some people liked to call the second Black Renaissance was coming to an end. Like the Harlem Renaissance of nearly half a century earlier, it had lasted about ten years and came to an end partly because the country went into an economic decline and partly because, as the writer Langston Hughes wrote about the Harlem Renaissance, "How could a large and enthusiastic group of people be crazy about Negroes forever?"

The second Black Renaissance had not started because a black show was a hit on Broadway, or because a new black music form had caught the fancy of the country. It had started as a result of the civil rights movement. The willingness of large numbers of black people, and their white supporters, to march and demonstrate and sit in and boycott in order to gain their rights made a profound impression on many white people, including those in power. In the 1960s, under President Lyndon B. Johnson, who became president after the assassination of President John F. Kennedy in November 1963, important laws were passed to help guarantee the rights that black people demanded. There was a Civil Rights Act and a Voting Rights Act, and although the southern states were not too happy about ending traditional segregation practices, they did slowly begin to bow to the law of the land. What many people called the New South was born, and in some parts of the South blacks were able to use their new right to vote to gain political power.

Having accomplished as much as they could, for the time being, in the South, civil rights leaders like Dr. Martin Luther King, Jr., turned their attention to other important causes. They looked to the North, where in many areas a more subtle form of segregation called de facto segregation was practiced. They pointed out that black people who lived in northern urban ghettos might as well live under segregation, because where they lived and where they went to school were separate from white neighborhoods and educational institutions. Dr. King and others also addressed themselves to the Vietnam War, which under President Johnson became a conflict in which the United States fully participated. A very strong antiwar movement developed among the young people in the country, and because young blacks were being drafted in larger numbers than young whites, many veterans of the civil rights movement naturally moved on to that cause. Others, like Dr. King, believed that the United States had no right to interfere in what they felt was another country's civil war.

On April 4, 1968, Dr. King was assassinated, and the civil rights movement came to an end. But the momentum of the movement continued on for a while without him. Although there were no more marches or major civil-rights campaigns, the civil-rights and voting laws had set into motion a strong emphasis on the part of the government to try to make up for past wrongs done to black people. President Johnson had launched a War on Poverty, and much of the money spent on this domestic war was earmarked for black-populated areas. Education acts made available money to libraries so they could buy more books about black people, and book publishers rushed to provide more books about blacks for the libraries to buy. Many rich white people and intellectual white people also gave money to black causes and supported the work of black writers and thinkers. Records by black teenage performers, especially those produced by Motown Records (then based in Detroit and the forerunner of Motown Productions) were bought not just by black teenagers but by white teenagers as well. There were more black dramatic plays and musicals on Broadway. And out in Hollywood, black films, especially action films, were being produced in numbers that Lena Horne, back in the 1930s, could not have imagined even in her wildest dreams.

The height of this second Black Renaissance occurred in the late 1960s–early 1970s, and much of it took place without Lena's participation. It began around the time that Dr. King was killed. Lena grieved over Dr. King's death, but in a short time she was also grieving over her father and her son. Both the elder Teddy Horne and the younger Teddy Jones were ill for some time before they actually died, and Lena was too involved in dealing, first, with their coming deaths, and then, with their actual deaths, to be able to think about outside things. It was Lennie's unexpected death that really caused her to question her ability to survive, and by the time she emerged from her mourning over Lennie's passing, on top of those of her father and son, the second Black Renaissance was already beginning to wind down.

She did not feel as if she had missed very much in terms of furthering her career. She had already established herself as a professional and did not need any short-lived renaissance to cause her to be in demand as a performer. In fact, she could have done many more important club appearances than she cared to do. She might have enjoyed the Hollywood renaissance for blacks, for in the new films black women tended to be gun-toting detectives and high-class fashion models and all kinds of other characters that were unheard of for blacks when Lena had first gone to Hollywood. But by the time Hollywood started producing these kinds of movies for blacks, Lena was well past the age when she would have been believable as either a pistol-packing detective or a fashion model, even if she was gorgeous and did not look her age.

Thus, it might be said that the second Black Renaissance passed Lena Horne by. On the other hand, it could also be said that she passed on it. She did not need it to put her before the American public or to establish her reputation. And when it ended, there was very little impact, if any, on her career.

Before, during, and after the second Black Renaissance, Lena continued to do what she wanted to do. She maintained her strong connection with Delta Sigma Theta over the years and offered her help in the various activities of the sorority. She did occasional benefits for causes she considered worthy. But she spent a lot of time relaxing and enjoying the rewards of having worked so hard for so many years. She bought another house in California, this one in Santa Barbara. A large, rambling house with a fieldstone exterior on an acre of land, it was a converted olive mill, and Lena loved planting orange trees and harvesting their fruit each year. It was a real haven for her, and she allowed only close friends and associates to visit her there.

Had she been willing, she could have received reporters nearly every day, especially reporters from women's magazines. Somehow, although she was in her sixties, she had retained the complexion and skin texture of a woman in her forties. Naturally, other women wanted to know her secret, and when Lena proved hard to interview the rumors were rife that she had lied about her birth date, or had had a face-lift, or *something*. Occasionally, Lena consented to talk about her "beauty secrets."

She didn't have any. When asked if she'd ever had a face-lift, she explained that her skin keloids, or forms excessive scar tissue, when cut. A face lift would have caused obvious and unsightly scars.

In 1980 Lena granted a rare interview to *Ebony* Magazine. Not only was it a fairly long interview, but it was also conducted at her Santa Barbara home, which had generally been off-limits to the press. But *Ebony* had been very kind to her over the years, including the years when she was not so well known; in fact, her picture on the cover of the issue that contained this interview was the tenth *Ebony* cover on which she had appeared. In the 1980 interview with *Ebony*, she made a startling admission: she had not actually loved Lennie Hayton when she had married him. She had respected him and admired his musical talent, but she had married him primarily because she was alone and had a family to support. "It was cold blooded and deliberate," she said. "I married him because he could get me into places a black man couldn't. But I really learned to love him. He was beautiful, just so damned good. I had never met a man like him."

What she did not tell the *Ebony* interviewer was that she considered this interview the last important interview she would give, because she was planning to retire. She had agreed to a two-month tour, and on the night of the first concert at the Ahmanson Theater in Los Angeles, on June 18, 1980, she announced that this concert was the beginning of a farewell tour that would end in August 1980, with her retirement from show business.

The tour, sponsored by Delta Sigma Theta, was hugely successful, and Lena's road manager, Sherman Sneed, believed that if Lena retired now she would be making a mistake. She was a living legend, and people wanted to see her; what's more, she had something to teach them about living. In August, Lena went back home to her gardens in Santa Barbara, California, but she agreed to let Sneed undertake negotiations for a one-woman show that he hoped to get on Broadway. In a few months' time he had secured the necessary financial backing and, equally important, the support of James Nederlander, whose family rivaled the Shuberts as powerful Broadway theater operators. Soon, Lena was planning her one-woman Broadway show.

Lena Horne: The Lady and Her Music opened at the Nederlander Theater on March 12, 1981, for a "limited engagement," and in the weeks that followed tickets to the show were the most sought-after on Broadway. Big-name stars and friends packed the house. Her daughter, Gail, and all five of Lena's grandchildren came. But except for them, Lena had no close family left. Her mother had died four years before, and Lena had never been able to reconnect with her the way she had with her father and her son before their deaths. She wondered what her mother would have thought of her daughter's one-woman show on Broadway, the culmination of all her dreams for both herself and her daughter.

Lena, standing alone in the spotlight on the Broadway stage, reflected Lena in real life: She was a one-woman show. There were two young dancers who accompanied her in some of the numbers she sang, and her orchestra conductor, Linda Twine, enjoyed a modicum of stardom because of the fact that there are very few women conductors on Broadway, and no other black ones. But Lena was essentially the entire show, commanding the stage and somehow transforming the large theater into an intimate spot, making each member of the audience feel as if she were addressing him or her only. She sang the songs that had long been associated with her, like "The Surrey with the Fringe on Top" and "Stormy Weather," and songs that conveyed the messages she wanted to put across, "If You Believe" and "I Got a Name." She sang songs with poignant personal meaning, like "Yesterday, When I Was Young" and "Life Goes

On." Interspersed with these songs were monologues about her life and career in which she talked easily to the audience about her experiences. So casual were these talks that they seemed more like dialogues and in fact are called that in the show's script and on the liner notes of the album of the show. She told about the slights she had experienced and of the hard times in Hollywood and at the Cotton Club, but she told about them with humor. There was not a single note of bitterness in her tone, only a deep sense of understanding. She was sharing her wisdom with the audience, and they responded with love. This was not a one-way show, everybody was involved.

The original limited engagement of the show was extended, and then extended again. Eight times a week the Nederlander Theater rocked with applause and thundered with standing ovations. The critics responded as enthusiastically as the audiences. *Lena Horne: The Lady and Her Music* and its star won a special Tony Award, a Drama Desk award, a citation from the Drama Critics' Circle, the Handel Medallion, two Grammy awards, and the Emergence Award, given by the Dance Theater of Harlem to public-spirited people whose achievements bring beauty and enrichment to all of humanity. The run of the show was extended again; altogether, it was extended four times and became the longest-running, one-woman show on Broadway.

At last, on June 30, 1982, the night of Lena's sixty-fifth birthday and her three hundred thirty-third sold-out performance, she took her final bows at the Nederlander Theater. But that was not the end of *Lena Horne: The Lady and Her Music*. Immediately, Lena began a national tour with the show, and there were plans to take it to Europe after that. At sixty-five, Lena seemed to be just getting started.

But although she was one of the few women who really did look twenty years younger, Lena was indeed sixty-five. It took time for her to get ready for her shows, and there was little energy left over for much other activity. She knew she would have to pace herself if she were to continue performing, and to give the kind of performance she felt her audiences deserved. Still, she had certain advantages over younger performers: *She* had nothing to prove. She was not putting everything she had into her show because she was aiming for even bigger things; she was doing it because at long last she didn't want to do anything else. She had finally opened up, to herself and to other people. She had finally connected with life. Ironically, it had been the death of her closest loved ones that had brought about this connection. "The pain of loss somehow cracked me open," she explains, "made me feel compassion."

Not until she was in her fifties did Lena Horne come to know herself and be herself. She admits that she is an extremely late bloomer and her advice to young people includes the admonition, "For heaven's sake, don't bloom as late as I did." But some people never bloom at all, never get out of the bud stage. And some people, like some flowers, bloom quickly and then fade. Lena Horne is like a hardy autumn perennial.

Index

Ahmanson Theater, 151
Alabama Club, 71
Allen, Steve, 109
Allyson, June, 106
Anderson, Eddie, 78, 112
Apollo Theater, 60–63, 68
Arlen, Harold, 38, 95, 113–114, 132
Armstrong, Louis, 33, 77
"As Long As I Live," 38
Atlanta, Ga., 25, 131
Augusta (cousin), 17, 19

Baldwin, James, 127–129
Barnet, Charlie, 61–65, 84
Barrymore, John, 71
Basie, Count, 65, 75, 119
Bates, Daisy, 89
Beatles, the, 138
Belafonte, Harry, 113, 127–128, 137–138
Belgium, 102
Bennett, Tony, 142–144
Bethune, Mary McLeod, 124
Beverly Hills Luau, 120–122

Birmingham, Ala., 125–127, 132
"Black Bird," 138
Black Hollywood: The Negro in Motion Pictures, 74
Blackbirds of 1939, 52–54, 60
Blacks
    in Hollywood, 51, 68–69, 73–74, 80, 87, 91, 149–150
    middle class, 11–13, 29, 33, 44, 56, 66–67, 86, 133
    racial and color prejudices of, 12, 17, 29, 33, 42, 62, 85, 103
    second Renaissance, 147, 149–150
    stereotyping of, in films and plays, 60, 72–73, 78, 80, 87, 95–96, 112, 115, 119–120
    in television, 109, 111–112
    See also Racial discrimination
Blake, Eubie, 41
Bogart, Humphrey, 80
Bontemps, Arna, 95
Boston, Mass., 43, 54, 90, 115, 142

Britain, 101, 134, 142
British Broadcasting Company
    (BBC), 112, 137
Broadway, 32, 39, 41, 52, 77, 95–
    96, 112–118, 139, 143, 152
Bronx, N.Y., 29–30, 61
Brooklyn, N.Y., 11, 13, 18–19, 22,
    27–29, 32–33, 35–36, 64,
    133
Brooklyn Ethical Culture School,
    16–17, 20
Buck and Bubbles, 77–78

Cabin in the Sky, 72, 74–81
Caesar's Palace, 138
Café Society Downtown, 65–68, 72,
    75
Café Society Uptown, 65, 68
Calloway, Cab, 32, 35–36, 76, 81,
    86
Canada, 142–143
Capitol Theater, 79
Carnegie Hall, 132–133
Carroll, Harrison, 74
Castro, Premier Fidel, 59
Catlin, Charlotte, 56–57
Charisse, Cyd, 138
Cincinnati, Oh., 45–46
Cinema Texas, 77
Circle Star Theater, 145
Civil rights movement, 117, 125–
    128, 130, 132, 136, 144,
    147–148
Clark, Dr. Kenneth, 127–128
Cleveland, Oh., 46–47
Club Champs-Elysée, 102
Club Trocadero, 68, 70–71
Clyde Beatty Circus, 45
Cocoanut Grove, the, 114
Cole, Nat King, 111
Comden, Betty, 132
"Come Rain or Come Shine," 95
Congress of Racial Equality
    (CORE), 125
Cooper, Ralph, 51
Copacabana, the, 100

Cotton Club, the, 31–41, 71, 79,
    91, 113, 143, 153
Cotton Club Parade, 39
Council for African Affairs, 108
Crane, Steve, 71
Crawford, Joan, 97
Cuba, 29–30, 86–87
Cullen, Countee, 95

Dailey, Dan, 138
Dance With Your Gods, 39
Daniels, Billie, 72, 75
Dean Martin Show, The, 138
Death of a Gunfighter, 138–140
Delta Sigma Theta (DST), 123–124,
    126–127, 132, 136, 138,
    150–151
"Didn't We," 138
Dietrich, Marlene, 71
"Dinner For One, Please, James,"
    42
Downs, Hugh, 131
Duke Is Tops, The, 51–52, 60, 77
Dunham, Katherine, and dancers,
    68, 71, 77, 81

Ebony Magazine, 151
Eckstine, Billy, 145
Ed Sullivan Show, The, 109
Edwina (cousin), 64, 69–70, 84–85,
    98–99
Ellington, Duke, 32, 36, 51, 60,
    68, 70–71, 73, 78–79
Ellington, Mercer, 131–132
England. *See* Britain
Ethical Culture Society, 3, 15
Europe, 101, 106, 108, 153. *See
    also* Belgium; Britain; etc.
Evers, Medgar, 130–132

Falana, Lola, 145
"Fine and Mellow," 67
Fitzgerald, Ella, 42, 60, 94
Fort Riley, Kan., 88–89
Fort Valley, Ga., 23–25
Francis Edwards Restaurant, 82

Franklin, Aretha, 145
Freed, Arthur, 77, 95

Garland, Judy, 106
George Washington Carver (ship), 88
Girls' High School, 28
Glasgow, Scotland, 108
"Good for Nothing Joe," 63, 65
Gordy, Berry, 146
Grable, Betty, 61
Grace, Bishop C. M. ("Daddy"), 107
Graham, Olive, 77
Great Depression, the, 30, 37
Green, Adolph, 132
Gregory, Dick, 130, 132
Gumm, Harold, 50, 52, 60, 68

Hammond, John, 65
Hampton, Lionel, 60
Hansberry, Lorraine, 127
Harburg, Yip, 113, 132
Harlem, 16, 30, 32, 34, 37, 39, 59, 61
   Renaissance, 32, 41, 147
   YWCA, 62
Harris, Ralph, 105, 144
Harris, Winonie, 71
Harvey, Georgette, 39
Hawkins, Assemblyman Gus, 80
Hayton, Lennie, 82–84, 86, 90, 96, 98–109, 115, 118, 120, 122, 134, 141–142, 144–145, 149, 151
Heflin, Van, 106
"Hello, Young Lovers," 138
Henderson, Fletcher, 88
Henderson, Horace, 88
Henderson, Luther, 101–102
Hernandez, Juano, 36
Holiday, Billie, 60, 63, 65–68
Hollywood, Ca., 50–51, 68–81, 85–87, 89, 91, 106, 119, 139–140, 149–150, 153
Hollywood Citizen-News, 114
Hollywood Independent Citizens

Committee of the Arts, Sciences, and Professions (HICCASP), 80, 108
Horne, Burke (uncle), 15, 28, 68
Horne, Cora Calhoun (grandmother), 11, 13–17, 24, 27–29, 49, 67, 69, 123–124, 135
Horne, Edna Scottron (mother). *See* Rodriguez, Edna
Horne, Edwin, Sr. (grandfather), 13–15, 24, 27–28, 53
Horne, Frank (uncle), 23–25, 68
Horne, Lena Calhoun
   appearance, 11–12, 20, 24, 31, 48–49, 60, 138, 150–151, 153
   awards, 153
   birth and early childhood, 11–17
   blacklisted, 107–109
   charities and causes, 87–90, 125–130, 136, 138
   as "different," 20, 22, 24, 35, 46, 94, 99, 103–104, 122–123, 130
   divorce, 90–91, 98
   marriages, 48, 100–103
   pregnancies, 49–50, 55
   racial attitudes, 46, 53, 63, 66–68, 76, 84, 99, 144
   schooling, 16–17, 20, 28–30, 33
Horne, Teddy (father), 12–16, 21, 24, 34, 46–47, 49, 55, 62, 72–73, 103, 134–135, 139–140, 142–143, 149
Howard Theater, 92–94
Howard University, 76
Hughes, Langston, 147

I Dood It, 82
"I Got a Name," 152
"If You Believe," 152
Ingram, Rex, 39, 77–78
Iturbi, José, 109

Jack Benny Show, The, 112
Jackson, Michael, 146

Jackson, Miss., 129–130, 132
Jamaica, 113, 115–119, 123, 127, 139
Janssen, David, 137
"Jim Crow," 19
Johnson, Erskine, 106
Johnson, President Lyndon B., 147–148
Johnson, Van, 106
Jones, Gail. *See* Lumet, Gail
Jones, Louis, 46–58, 60, 64, 68, 79, 85, 90–91, 135
Jones, Teddy, 55, 58, 64, 68, 72, 84–85, 90–91, 108, 112, 135, 138–140, 142–143, 149
Josephson, Barney, 65–69, 75, 81
Jump for Joy, 71
Junior Debs, 35

Kelly, Gene, 106
Kennedy, Attorney General Robert F., 127–129
Kennedy, President John F., 128, 147
King, Dr. Martin Luther, Jr., 125–126, 131, 148–149
Koehler, Ted, 38
Kraft Music Hall, 138
Kyle, Tiny, 101

Lafayette Players, 16
Las Vegas, Nev., 110, 135, 138
Lena Horne: The Lady and Her Music, 152–153
Leslie, Lew, 52–56, 60, 115
Lewis, Bobby, 116
"Life Goes On," 152
Life Magazine, 76
"Life's Full of Consequences," 80
Little Troc, the, 71–72
Loew's Theaters, 87, 91–92, 96
London Casino, 101
"Loneliness," 143
Long, Avon, 38
Lorre, Peter, 80
Los Angeles, Ca., 70, 143, 151

Los Angeles Daily News, 106
Los Angeles Herald Examiner, 121
Los Angeles Sentinel, 92–94
Los Angeles Times, 133, 140
Louis, Joe, 46, 74–75
   Louis–Schmeling fight, 46
Lumet, Amy, 134
Lumet, Gail Jones, 50, 52, 54–55, 57–58, 64, 69–70, 84–85, 108, 112, 134, 138, 141, 145, 152
Lumet, Sidney, 134, 145–146
Lunceford, Jimmie, 36, 91–92
Lyles, Aubrey, 41

McCarthy, Senator Joseph, 107
McDaniel, Hattie, 73–74
Macon, Ga., 22–23
McShann, Jay, 60
Madden, Owney, 31–32, 34, 39–40, 42
"Man I Love, The," 66
March on Washington, 132
Marshall, Burke, 128
Mayer, Louis B., 72, 77, 97, 99
Meet Me in Las Vegas, 138
Mercer, Johnny, 95
Meredith, James, 128
Metro-Goldwyn-Mayer (M-G-M), 72, 74–75, 77, 80–82, 87, 90–91, 95–96, 98, 100, 104, 106–107, 133, 138–139
Miami, Fla., 19–21
Miller, Flournoy, 41
Mills, Florence, 15, 53
Minnelli, Vincente, 72, 74, 80, 82
Monsanto Night Presents Lena Horne, 137
Montgomery, Ala., bus boycott, 125
Mosby, Aline, 114
Motown Productions, 146, 149
Music Corporation of America (MCA), 97, 99–100, 105

National Association for the Advancement of Colored People (NAACP), 15–16, 29, 44,

52, 69, 73, 89, 95, 125,
129–131, 133
National Broadcasting Company
(NBC), 111, 131, 137
National Council of Negro Women,
124, 136, 138
National Urban League, 29
Nederlander, James, 152
Nederlander Theater, 152–153
New York, N.Y., 59–61, 64, 71, 75,
79, 86, 100, 107, 112, 116–
117, 142–143
New York Times, 13, 137
Nicholas Brothers, 81
Nichols Canyon (Ca.), 96, 104
Noble, Jean, 123–127, 130
"Now," 132–133
Null, Gary, 74, 80

O'Neill, Zulme, 76
Orpheum Theater, 91–92

Palm Springs, Ca., 126, 145
Panama Hattie, 74, 78
Paramount Theater, 64
Paris, France, 101–102, 106, 109
Parker, Charlie "Yardbird," 60
Perry Como Show, The, 109
Philadelphia, Pa., 19, 41–43
Piccadilly Hotel, 101
Pittsburgh, Pa., 47–48, 52, 54, 57–
58, 62, 64, 68
Pompton Lakes, N.J., 46
Prohibition, 31, 37

Queens, N.Y., 86–87, 104

Racial discrimination and segregation, 12, 19, 42–43, 46, 48–
50, 63, 65–69, 74–76, 78,
80, 85–86, 88–90, 92, 99–
100, 103–106, 119–120,
125, 128, 132–133, 148
Radcliffe College, 112, 134
Raphaël Hotel, 101–102
Red Channels, 108–109, 111
Richmond, June, 92

Ritz-Carlton Hotel, 43
Robeson, Paul, 67, 69, 108–109
Robinson, Bill "Bojangles," 81
Robinson, Clarence, 61–62
Rodriguez, Edna Scottron, 11, 13–
14, 16–23, 25–31, 33–36,
38–39, 41–42, 44–45, 47,
49, 55–56, 72, 86–87, 135,
152
Rodriguez, Miguel, 29–30, 38–45,
47, 55, 61, 66, 86–87
Rollock, Mrs. Laura, 28–29, 31–32,
49
Roosevelt, Mrs. Eleanor, 124
Roosevelt, President Franklin D.,
24, 68
Ross, Diana, 146
Rutgers University, 67

St. Louis Woman, 95–96
St. Vincent, Harvey, 121–122
San Francisco, Ca., 145
Sands Hotel, 138
Santa Barbara, Ca., 150–151
Savoy Plaza Hotel, 75–76, 90, 102
Scott, Hazel, 67–68, 81–83
Shaw, Artie, 62–63, 65, 83
Shore, Dinah, 61, 65
Shubert Theaters, 143, 152
Shuffle Along, 41
"Silent Spring," 132–133
Sinatra, Frank, 132
Sing Sing prison, 137
Sissle, Noble, 41–47, 53, 60–61
Skelton, Red, 74
"Sleepy Time Down South," 65–66
Smith, Jerome, 128–129
Smith, O. C , 137
Sneed, Sherman, 144–145, 151–
152
Sokolsky, George, 109
Sothern, Ann, 74
Southern Christian Leadership Con-
ference (SCLC), 125, 131
"Stardust," 62, 83
Starks, Mrs. Ida, 85–87
Stockholm, Sweden, 108

Stormy Weather (film), 81–82
"Stormy Weather" (song), 81, 137, 143, 152
Strayhorn, Billy, 71–73, 75, 130
Student Nonviolent Coordinating Committee (SNCC), 125, 128, 132–133
Sullivan, Ed, 109
"Surrey with the Fringe on Top, The," 138, 152

"Taking a Chance on Love," 80
Terre Haute, Ind., 45
Theresa Hotel, 59–60, 62, 75–76
Thomas, Dylan, 101
Thomas, Kevin, 140
Thompson, Kay, 82, 120
Till the Clouds Roll By, 106
Time Magazine, 76
Today Show, The, 131
Tonight Show, The, 109
Torn, Rip, 127
Turner, Lana, 71
Turner, Mrs. (babysitter), 58
Twentieth Century-Fox, 81
Twine, Linda, 152
Two Girls and a Sailor, 106

United Service Organization (USO), 87–89
United States
    Air Force, 99th Squadron, 88

Army, 74, 85, 88–89
University of Mississippi, 128

Victoria Theatre, 61
Vietnam War, 129, 148

Waldorf-Astoria Hotel, 112–113
Waller, Fats, 81
Warga, Wayne, 137
Warwick, Dionne, 145
Washington, D.C., 63
Waters, Ethel, 36, 68, 77–79
Webb, Chick, 42
Webb, Jimmy, 138
West Virginia State College, 47
White, Josh, 67
White, Walter, 69, 119, 133
Widmark, Richard, 138, 140
Wilkins, Roy, 131
Williams, Paul, 143
Wilson, Dooley, 82
Wilson, Lucille, 33
Wilson, Mary, 145
Windsor Theater, 61
Wiz, The, 146
Words and Music, 106
World War II, 71, 76, 87, 102

"Yesterday, When I Was Young," 152
Young, Felix, 68, 70–71